D0485883

You Shouldnt Have!

You Shouldn't Have!

HOW TO GIVE GIFTS THEY'LL NEVER FORGET

LEAH INGRAM

Contemporary Books

Chicago   New York   San Francisco   Lisbon   London   Madrid   Mexico City
Milan   New Delhi   San Juan   Seoul   Singapore   Sydney   Toronto

Library of Congress Cataloging-in-Publication Data

Ingram, Leah.
    You shouldn't have! : how to give gifts they'll never forget / Leah Ingram.
       p.   cm.
    ISBN 0-8092-9326-9
    1. Gifts—Planning.   I. Title.

GT3040. I54   2001
394—dc21   2001025388

Contemporary Books

A Division of The **McGraw-Hill** *Companies*

Copyright © 2002 by Leah Ingram. All rights reserved. Printed in the United States of America. Except as permitted under the United States Copyright Act of 1976, no part of this publication may be reproduced or distributed in any form or by any means, or stored in a database or retrieval system, without the prior written permission of the publisher.

1 2 3 4 5 6 7 8 9 0   AGM/AGM   0 9 8 7 6 5 4 3 2 1

ISBN 0-8092-9326-9

This book was set in Electra
Printed and bound by Quebecor Martinsburg

Cover and interior design by Kim Bartko
Cover photo courtesy Sardi Klein

McGraw-Hill books are available at special quantity discounts to use as premiums and sales promotions, or for use in corporate training programs. For more information, please write to the Director of Special Sales, Professional Publishing, McGraw-Hill, Two Penn Plaza, New York, NY 10121-2298. Or contact your local bookstore.

This book is printed on acid-free paper.

CONTENTS

Acknowledgments

I love everything having to do with gift giving. I love shopping for gifts, I love receiving gifts, and I even enjoy writing thank-you notes to those who've given me gifts. I don't think I would have developed my love, or expertise, had it not been for my family, who have always been generous with gifts to me—especially my mother, Judy Ingram, and my husband, William Behre. In addition, my children, Jane and Anne, have given me a newfound appreciation for kids' gifts—and been the inspiration for many gifts I've given others, especially their grandparents.

Many thanks to my agent, Linda Konner, and editor Betsy Lancefield, both of whom believed in this book as enthusiastically as I did, as well as Deborah Durham, who encouraged me to pursue a gift-giving book. A special thanks goes out to Linda Daily Paulson, who helped me track down off-beat gift ideas from around the country. I'm confident its publication will bring only good things to all of us—and great gift ideas for our friends and families—in the future.

Finally, thank you to the friends I've made through membership in the American Society of Journalists and Authors and in the National Writers Union, as well as on Jforum and the various listserves to which I subscribe. Many of you shared stories of wonderful gifts you've given and received, and without your spirited anecdotes, parts of this book would not have come to life.

INTRODUCTION

Gift giving is something we face every day and throughout our lives—from the holiday present we give our long-ago first-grade teacher to the "thanks for the business" gift we gave a client. My daughter Jane was less than a year old when she gave her first gift, albeit with my help. It was a T-shirt for her dad that featured Jane's footprints and said "My daddy lets me walk all over him." Jane and I made it together (OK, I painted the bottoms of Jane's feet with fabric paint and helped her "walk" across the shirt), and we gave it to my husband for Father's Day.

The gift itself took less than ten minutes to make, and probably less than $10 for supplies, but it was a gift he truly loved and still loves: it was from his daughter and his wife, it had great sentiment attached to it, and it was something that—I believed—a T-shirt lover such as my husband would really appreciate. I know I was right because he still proudly wears that shirt nearly six years later—and to this day, he still gives me specific laundering instructions for it (no bleach, not too long in the dryer) because he wants it to last for a long time.

In my opinion, this simple gift has the elements that make it a great gift: it was geared toward the recipient's likes (he's a world-class T-shirt guy), and it had personal meaning for him (what dad wouldn't love something that his child helped to make, especially on his first Father's Day?). Of course, it's easy for me to analyze my own performance in this regard, since I've spent the past few years developing my gift-giving expertise, and I know the hows and whys of the gifts I give. What I hope to do is help you to become a great gift giver, too. Obviously, you're ready for some help, or you wouldn't be reading this book.

Rules of Gift Giving

Now, I know how stressful giving a gift can be — especially when you stop to consider how many gifts we give each year. A recent Lenox Company study showed that the average American buys forty-seven gifts annually! If you enjoy gift giving as I do, you probably give many more gifts than that, and it would seem that you'd run out of original ideas pretty quickly. However, that doesn't have to be the case.

If you know how to approach your gift giving and what techniques you can use to determine the best gift to give someone for a certain occasion, giving gifts will get a lot easier. There are four basic rules that I believe can be applied to any gift-giving situation and steer you to the right choice. You'll come across them again throughout the book. Here they are:

Know the Occasion and Your Recipient

You wouldn't buy your boss some lingerie to congratulate her on her promotion, nor would a man delight his wife with a silver pen on Valentine's Day. But switch the situations, and the gifts make perfect sense. It may seem utterly obvious that lingerie doesn't mix with the office—but you would be surprised: Many, many people don't stop to think about the occasion for which they're giving a gift, as well as the recipient, before they make a purchase.

Do your homework before you start shopping. Ask questions of those who've gone before. Find out what is and isn't part of the culture in your social or work setting. Prompt people for examples of presents that have brought down the house in the past—and ones that bombed so miserably that you'll know to avoid them at all costs. Then, once you have a good sense of the dos and don'ts for the gift-giving situation, you can start shopping with confidence.

Consider Your Budget

The fact that your brother makes a million dollars on Wall Street doesn't mean that you need to spend megabucks on gifts for him. You shouldn't ever feel that you must equate the value of your gift to the recipient's household income. Gear your gift toward your own budget and what feels right to you. You don't want to come away from any gift-giving situation feeling that you spent too much. Decide ahead of time approximately how much you would like to spend on the gift, and do your best not to veer from this figure.

Whenever Possible, Personalize the Gift

When I say "personalize" a gift, I'm not saying pay extra to have that scarf monogrammed, although monogrammed gifts make a wonderful impression. The point here is to choose a gift that will feel personal to the recipient—because, ideally, it is related to a favorite hobby or activity. I once read some sage advice that admonished against giving people what you'd like to receive, as a hint for future gift-giving occasions. Rather, you should think about what that person likes to do in his or her free time and then use this information to guide your choice.

One year, my husband gave me a new camera for a Christmas present. You may think that a camera is a ho-hum gift, but I certainly wasn't yawning when I opened it. I've always been a bit of a shutterbug. I was the photo editor of my high school yearbook, spent hours in the darkroom at college, and once worked as a freelance photographer in New York City. However, after we had kids, it was impossible to drag around all of my professional equipment to take impromptu pictures, so I stopped taking pictures altogether. My husband knew how much I missed this activity, so he also knew that buying me a pocket-size camera that had all the features of my other equipment but without the bulk was the perfect gift for me.

Don't Reinvent the Wheel

Sometimes out of pure luck, you hit the gift-giving jackpot. You give your mother-in-law a gift that you figured she'd like, and instead of just liking it, she's in seventh heaven. Not only does she tell everyone who'll listen what a swell gift you gave her, but she also writes you one of the most heartfelt thank-you notes you've ever received. If this has happened to you on a certain occasion, then I say, Don't mess with success. That is, if a certain kind of gift worked in the past for a certain person, give it again. And again. There's no reason you should tax yourself at each birthday or holiday by trying to reinvent the gift-giving wheel.

Of course, if that winning gift is the pearl necklace you gave your sister for her birthday last year, logically you wouldn't give her another pearl necklace this year. But you can give her accessories to go along with the necklace, such as matching earrings, a pearl pin, or even a new jewelry box. The next time you find yourself in need of a gift—but stumped as to what to buy—keep these four tips in mind. You're sure to find a great gift.

You Shouldn't Have!

Gift Giving FYI

When it comes to wrapping gifts, Americans use a lot of wrapping paper—nearly seven regular-sized rolls for holiday gifts alone, according to a new survey by 3M, the makers of Scotch brand tapes. However, when we run out of wrapping paper, we don't all run to the store; Americans tend to complete the gift-wrapping job with whatever they find around the house. According to the same 3M survey, here are some of the gift-wrapping alternatives we use, as well as the percentage of people who turn to these offbeat wrapping resources. Next time you run short of paper, you may consider:

paper or plastic bags	28%
newsprint	24%
tissue paper	15%
comics	14%
plastic wrap	6%
aluminum foil	5%
discarded yellow pages	1%

---

the wheel, so to speak, each year—especially when it comes to holidays and birthdays.

Of course, this rule applies only when you're certain that the recipients genuinely like what you gave them. So, ask—and tell them to be honest with you. This lets people know that you care enough to give them the best gift. If your last gift didn't bowl them over, ask what they would like instead. Solicit a couple of ideas, make note of them, and then choose one of these items for the next occasion. As always, stick with suggestions that fall within your price range. A brand-new Hummer is probably a bit much to come through with, but you could give the Matchbox version for a gag gift. Whichever way you lean, now that you've got the information right from the source—the prospective recipient—you can feel confident that you'll be giving a much-wanted gift next year, and for years to come.

Q: Is it ever OK to give cash as a gift?

A: I believe cash, or its equivalent in the form of a gift certificate or gift card, is appropriate in many situations. So, you shouldn't feel awkward about the practice of giving cash as a gift. My children's grandparents often send a crisp $5 or $10 bill for the kids' birthdays or as part of their Christmas gifts, and the girls are awed by getting "real" money. Religious celebrations such as bar mitzvahs are also times when you should have no qualms about giving cash, as are graduations from high school or college. And if cash gifts are acceptable in your social circle as wedding gifts (as they are on the East Coast where I grew up), by all means write the bride and groom a check.

On similar occasions, a cash equivalent will be graciously accepted. You can buy a savings bond upon the birth of a child, or a gift certificate from a home-decor or hardware retailer for a housewarming. For example, my mother gave my husband and me two $100 Home Depot gift cards when we moved into our house. They were one of the most practical and used housewarming gifts we received.

If you want to get a little creative with your money gift, why not package it in a fun container? For instance, if you want to give money to a newly married couple or new home owners, place it in a watering can and include a card that says you hope this gift will help them sow the seeds of a happy life together—or something like that. (Make sure you're clear to the recipients that there is something inside the watering can before they put it to use.) For a kid going off to college, you can put the money in a take-out food container (available at craft stores in a variety of colors), and write a card that says you hope the student will use this money to help fund those late-night munching sessions with roommates. Have some fun with the packaging, and you'll end up giving a practical gift that will be fondly remembered.

Q: What are some good alternatives to taking a bottle of wine when you are invited to someone's house for dinner?

A: I think a bottle of wine is always welcomed when you're invited for dinner—that is, unless you know that the hosts have an alcohol dependency. Then, it would be in bad taste. You'll hear me saying this a lot:

❧ The Best Gift 1 Ever Got ❧

My daughter has a genetic disease that was diagnosed when she was two. Before we knew what was wrong with her, she was very sick, and my husband and I spent a lot of time at the hospital and away from home. One of the best gifts we received arrived shortly after all three of us came home: my coworkers, who had been wonderfully supportive throughout this ordeal, arranged to have dinner delivered to our apartment from our favorite restaurant—not only the first night we were home, but for a full week. I never remember food tasting so good as it did that first night. I truly appreciated this gift.

Jeanne, New York

> ### ⤞ *The Best Gift I Ever Gave* ⤝
>
> When a friend of mine needed an operation and then spent a few weeks recuperating at home, I sent him a Wolferman's gift basket filled with breakfast goodies—muffins, scones, coffee, and tea. I also send this kind of basket to families after a funeral as a "thinking of you" gift.
>
> *Margie, Massachusetts*

there's no reason to reinvent the wheel each time you must give someone a gift, including taking something for dinner. My friends know that I love white wine, so if they show up with a bottle of Pinot Grigio (my favorite) each time we invite them to dinner, I'm in heaven. I don't expect them to change what they bring, and I'm glad my friends are comfortable coming to dinner with the same wine each time.

However, if for some reason you feel you must take something different to dinner every once and awhile, why not try a twist on the bottle-of-wine approach and instead take a bottle of sparkling cider? This beverage is available in abundance during the fall. Or how about taking an appetizer or a dessert? (Of course, check with the hosts first; they may have dinner so impeccably planned that any additional foodstuff would throw things off balance.) There is a French bakery in our town called C'est La Vie that is truly *magnifique* and makes sublime desserts. Whenever we go to someone's house for dinner, if we're not taking wine, we visit this shop and pick up a scrumptious pear tart or some meringue cookies.

The Best All-Occasion Gifts

One of the most awkward situations to find yourself in is needing to give a last-minute gift but not having anything on hand that qualifies. You can avoid this fate by keeping a treasure trove of all-occasion gifts at your home at all times. A friend of mine calls it her gift closet. The best way to stock this stash is by purchasing potential gift items all year long, especially when you see them on sale at your favorite store.

Recently, I was shopping for back-to-school supplies at Staples when what to my wondering eyes should appear but a score of cute plastic picture frames in vibrant hues of green apple, bubble gum, and grape. Besides being eye-catching, they'd been marked down to less than two bucks each. Needless to say, I bought all twenty of them, and now I'm set for any gift "emergency" for which a colorful picture frame is appropriate.

The clearance aisle at your favorite retailer isn't the only place to seek out bargains. You can usually get some good buys at an outlet store, and even deep discounts if you time it right. Last month, my local Van Heusen outlet had men's ties on sale for $9, a tempting deal. And last year, Nordstrom Rack (the outlet version of Nordstrom department store) had notepaper with whimsical watercolor drawings on sale for about $2 per pack of eight. You can be sure I racked up a bunch. If you live near an outlet center, make it a practice to check in often so that you can catch the specials.

Gift cards and gift certificates can also serve their turn as last-minute gifts. Stores, businesses, and even restaurants sometimes offer customers a gift card or certificate in a moderate denomination as an incentive to return, and this is an excellent, free way of picking up one or more for your trove. Case in point: My family and I recently had lunch at the Rainforest Café. Along with our bill came a discount coupon for the Rainforest Store, which is adjacent to the Café. If we spent a certain amount of money in the store, we would receive two $25 gift certificates to the restaurant. Shopping trips to stores such as Target and Old Navy yielded similar benefits: because we spent a certain amount in those stores that day, we received $10 gift cards gratis.

As you can see, it's easy to be prepared even when you're taken by surprise. Stock up on the following great all-occasion gifts, and you won't get caught holding the bag:

1. Picture frames
2. Notepaper
3. Vases
4. Bath products
5. Kids' art supplies
6. Men's ties
7. Gift cards or certificates from local stores or businesses
8. High-end pens
9. Packages of golf balls and tees
10. Portable tool kits (such as a Swiss Army knife or Leatherman multi-purpose tool)

Q: I have a friend whose family earns a lot more than mine does, and she's always giving me extravagant gifts that I know cost a lot. I always feel bad when I give her something, because I'm afraid she'll look down on me and my gift for not meeting her standards. Should I blow my budget and buy her something really extravagant, too?

A: If this person who gives you such expensive gifts each year is a really good friend, I doubt she even stops to consider the value of the gifts you give her. I'm sure she's thrilled that you and she are close enough to exchange gifts and simply appreciates the sentiment with which the gifts are given. And that's the way gift giving should be. Now, if the person does comment on the value of the gift or where you got it, then maybe you need to reconsider whether you want to be exchanging gifts with this person at all. But that's a judgment call on your part.

As I said in the Introduction, one of my rules is that you should never take the recipient's salary into account when buying a gift. If someone always buys you something from an upscale store, you shouldn't feel compelled to do your shopping there as well. Rather, you should give something that suits your own budget and about which you feel good giving.

Q: How do I handle gift-giving occasions when I'm no longer close to someone? Do I still need to send gifts each birthday or holiday?

A: No. It is so normal for friendships to wax and wane that, for the sake of your financial stability and your own sanity, you need to readdress your gift list each year. Figure out the people to whom you no longer want to send gifts, for whatever reason that may be, and either remove them from your list completely or "wean" them off. In the latter case, instead of sending a gift for a birthday or holiday, send a card with a personal note in it. See if they respond in kind at your birthday or at Christmas. If they don't, then the following year, you can delete them entirely. If you don't hear from people at traditional occasions such as a birthday or holiday, you have to accept that the friendship has run its course and you need to let it go. However, if it feels right to continue sending a greeting at the holidays, by all means do so. Just don't make yourself crazy buying and sending gifts to someone you no longer communicate with regularly.

Here's a model you can follow to keep yourself organized so that you're not wasting money on cards or gifts for people from whom you've grown apart over time. Each December when I buy a new week-at-a-glance calendar insert for my Filofax, I take an hour or so to enter the birthdays and anniversaries of my friends and family members and their kids. I write the person's name on the date of his or her birthday or anniversary and, if I have the information, how old the person will be or what anniversary it is. Then about twice a month, I look through the coming weeks to see if there are any birthdays for which I need to send cards and/or gifts. Since I stock up on birthday cards (I save money by buying when the price is right and always have cards on hand), I usually only have to open a filing cabinet drawer to get a card. If I'm sending a gift, and if I don't want to raid the stash in my gift closet, I'll plan to do the necessary shopping and shipping well in advance.

Over the years, I've accepted that the roster of people with whom I'm close will change. There are friends and relatives whose birthdays or anniversaries I'd previously jotted in my calendar. But now, because of the passing of time or the fact that we no longer stay in touch, I don't feel the need to commemorate special occasions with a gift or a card.

For example, when my husband was attending graduate school, we lived in university family housing, which was actually glorified army barracks. Because of the tight quarters there, we couldn't help but become close with the families who lived nearby. All of our children played together, and we would exchange cards and gifts on birthdays and holidays. When members of the informal group slowly started moving away and taking jobs in different parts of the country, we kept up with the gift exchange for the first year or two. Then it transitioned to just cards. Now we may send an occasional E-mail message just to say "Hello," and each year we exchange holiday greetings. However, I no longer write the names and birthdays of these long-ago friends and their children in my calendar because the friendships have simply run their course, and I'm OK with that.

Are you feeling weighted down by the gift buying and card sending with which you're saddled at each birthday and holiday? If so, then I say

---

Would You Like That Gift-Wrapped?

If you ever stressed out about how to wrap a certain gift, imagine what people throughout history had to confront when presenting the following very large tokens:

- In 1912, Japan presented the then first lady Helen Herron Taft with more than three thousand cherry trees of twelve varieties to be planted in Washington, D.C.'s tidal basin. Those trees still stand today and are the central feature of Washington's famous Cherry Blossom Festival.

- Muslim emperor Shah Jahan of India had the Taj Majal built as a gift for his wife, Queen Mumtaz Majal. It is made entirely of white marble. It took twenty-two years to complete—unfortunately, Queen Majal died before it was done.

- France gave the American people the Statue of Liberty as a gift. Frédéric-Auguste Bartholdi designed and presented it in 1886. In order for it to get here, though, it had to be dismantled piece by piece, shipped in large crates to New York, and then reassembled on Liberty Island in New York Harbor.

---

that's a sign that you need to reevaluate the state of your friendships and see if it makes sense to hold off on gifts and just send cards to certain people. Or, if someone has never reciprocated or even acknowledged your generosity, you may want to stop sending anything at all. You'll make your load lighter in the long run if you do so.

Q: Is it ever inappropriate to send a gift when you find out that someone is sick or in the hospital? What about when someone dies?

A: For some reason, people are often hesitant to acknowledge when bad things happen in someone's life. I don't know if they think that it's bad manners or bad luck to discuss illness or death, but in my opinion, it's extremely bad manners not to at least acknowledge that something has happened. At a minimum, you should send a handwritten note to the sick person or the survivor to say that you're thinking of him or her and that you send your best wishes. You don't have to gush or go on and on about how sorry you are. A few brief but heartfelt lines are all that's necessary.

That's exactly what I did recently when I found out that a friend had suffered a miscarriage. I wrote a three-line note to tell her that while I had no idea what she and her husband must be going through, I wanted her to know that I was thinking of them. I hope that the note provided her with some comfort during that very difficult time.

Most people tend to send flowers when someone is sick or recovering from the death of a loved one. Flowers are a fine all-occasion gift (even if the occasion is one steeped in sadness), but sometimes you want your gift to be more than pretty. For these times, if you give something that will make the person's life easier during the recovery—such as food or assistance—you'll have given something truly special.

For instance, a thoughtful gift to send to someone who has just returned home from a hospital stay or a funeral is a few days' worth of homemade frozen meals. Package them in serving-size containers so that they can be popped into the microwave for an easy-to-fix, hot repast. If time or distance won't allow you to prepare and deliver the meals yourself, have a local restaurant or catering company send some from its menu.

Another gift that will help make life easier is to arrange for a cleaning service to visit the person's home on a regular basis. That way, housecleaning will be one less chore for your friend to worry about. One caveat to this suggestion: There are certain people for whom cleaning is therapeutic, and offering to have someone else perform the act may be seen as an intrusion. If you suspect this person is a cleaning-equals-therapy type, go with something else, such as food.

For a family with small children, a wonderful gift is the offer of free baby-sitting. You can suggest transporting the children to your own home to give the recovering person some quiet time, or just taking the kids out to lunch and a movie during the weekend. If you have a network of like-minded friends, belong to a play group, or are involved in a baby-sitting co-op, you can arrange it so that the family in need has enough baby-sitters lined up for days or weeks.

Whichever you choose, it will be a gift that is much appreciated.

A BABY IS BORN

Becoming a parent is one of the most exciting events in a person's life—whether the baby's arrival is via adoption or pregnancy. I have two children, and I can't imagine what life would be like without my daughters. What helped me get in the spirit of becoming a mother each time were the wonderful gifts that family and friends bestowed on my husband, Bill, and me during those very long nine months of gestation. I loved that people close to us didn't wait until our little bundle of joy arrived to give us gifts—although many showered us with good tidings after the births as well.

If you learn that a friend, family member, or work colleague is pregnant—and you know she's sharing the good news publicly—then feel free to give her a gift right away to celebrate the happy news. Late in my pregnancy with my first daughter, an ultrasound confirmed that Jane would be a Jane and not a John. We shared the news with our neighbors, with whom we'd grown close. The next day, they came by to deliver a small wrapped box, which contained a tiny porcelain statue of an angel holding a sign that said "It's a girl." That figurine probably cost no more than $5, but it meant a million to us because it was the first time someone had memorialized that we were going to have a daughter. I treasure that statue, and it became a fixture in the nursery after Jane was born and then in the room she shared with her sister, Anne, after she came along. Today, Jane is in elementary school, and the angel still holds a place of honor along with other prized possessions in her bedroom.

The Gift of Literature

Another class of while-you're-pregnant gifts that Bill and I received—and which I heartily recommend—is books on becoming a parent. One of

---

⊷ The Best Gift I Ever Got ⊷

At my baby shower, my best friend gave me a beautiful, black-and-white cotton kimono to wear when I was nursing (or any time, just to be comfortable). What was so striking about this was that all the other gifts were for the baby, but this one was for me. A number of years later, I did something similar for a friend having a baby shower: I gave her luxurious body creams and shampoos instead of baby T-shirts and booties. She loved the gift for the same reason I loved the kimono.

Susan, New York

Gift Giving FYI

Many families like to keep a copy of the newspaper from the day their children were born. If you live far away from a friend or relative who just had a baby, why not send a copy of your local paper from the big day? It will provide a different perspective on that day's news and add to the child's collection of mementos.

---

our favorites was a compilation of the comic strip "Baby Blues," which chronicles the ups and downs of being a parent. This book, called *I Saw Elvis in My Ultrasound*, is all about the hilarious antics of preparing for baby number two, and it was an ideal gift when I was pregnant with our second daughter.

Besides giving us material to enjoy together, some friends purchased books with just one of us in mind. Bill received several humorous books from friends and family on becoming a father, such as Bill Cosby's *Fatherhood* and Paul Reiser's *Babyhood*. These books became permanent fixtures on the nightstand and made for great before-bed reading. For me, the best parenting book I received was Anne Lamott's *Operating Instructions*.

Books for the Mother-to-Be

To date, I've probably read *Operating Instructions* at least five times. It is one of my all-time favorite books. In this pint-size paperback, you become immersed in Lamott's struggle during her son's first year to adapt to life not only as a parent but as a single parent as well. You get the lowdown on being up all night, breastfeeding hits and misses, and how it is that new mothers sometimes go for days without bathing. Some

> ⇜ *The Best Gift 1 Ever Got* ⇝
>
> After my third child was born, a friend brought over a gift, which I assumed would be some kind of clothing or toy for the baby. Imagine how delighted I was when I discovered it was a gift for *me*: a basket filled with scented soaps, lotions, and more.
>
> *Melanie, Wisconsin*

sections are laugh-out-loud funny; other parts are so poignant that you can't help but be moved. This book was so instrumental in helping me accept that being a parent is a crazy combination of flawed and funny moments that it is now my standard "congratulations on becoming pregnant" gift. I usually send a copy as soon as someone announces she's expecting.

While *Operating Instructions* is my parenting book of choice, plenty of other titles out there would also fill the bill. Is there a book that has meant a lot to you as a parent? If so, send a copy as a gift when someone you care about shares the good news. Remember: new parents—even those welcoming a subsequent child—are ravenous for information on what it's really like to assume the role.

Typically, within days of seeing that little line on the pregnancy test that tells a woman she's with child, she runs to a bookstore to scope out the complete *What to Expect . . .* series, plus any other titles that seem germane. Then, she usually loads up on subscriptions to parenting magazines so that she'll be 100 percent prepared for the big birth day. You can help build the library through your gift. Here are some off-the-shelf suggestions:

Insert an Inscription

You can add a special touch to a gift of a book by writing a heartfelt inscription inside the cover. If the book has personal meaning to you, mention that in your note. For example, for a close friend with a good sense of humor, you can write something like "This book gave me hours of entertainment (and some good parenting information to boot) and helped me forget how many times I'd just thrown up in the toilet."

Give an Autographed Copy

Another way to make your selection more meaningful requires some planning, but if you can pull it off, the gift will be worth the time. Find out if the author of your favorite book for expectant parents is coming to

---

❧ The Best Gift I Ever Gave ❧

When I was pregnant with number three, my sister was pregnant with her first. Since I couldn't be there for her baby shower, I decided to give her a shower by mail. I had everyone mail me the gifts they intended to give her, then I put them all in a huge box and had her shower delivered to her. Unbeknownst to me, my sister was planning the same thing. One day, my friend and her husband dropped by unexpectedly. They came bearing balloons, flowers, gifts, and a cake—all sent courtesy of my sister.

Barb, Kentucky

your town or a town near you for a book signing (look for lists of events at the bookstore or in the newspaper). Then, at the signing, buy a stack of those books and have the author autograph them. Now, when you give the book as a gift, it will be even more valuable.

This is exactly what I did a few years back when Anne Lamott was going to be in my town for a book signing. I bought ten copies of *Operating Instructions* and had Lamott sign her name to each. (I even took along my own dog-eared copy for her to sign as well.) Then, whenever one of my friends announced she was going to have a baby, I sent an author-signed version of the book. Sadly, my supply ran out this year, so I'm keeping my eyes and ears open for future Anne Lamott signings in my area.

Books to Avoid

While I fully endorse giving books about becoming a parent, I believe there are two categories of baby books that should be left for the new parents to get for themselves. They are baby-naming books and a child's baby book.

When I was pregnant with my children, Bill and I had a certain criteria for choosing our child's name. We didn't want anyone to influence us in our decision and therefore were particular about the name books we consulted. If anyone had purchased a baby-naming book for us, we would have felt that the person was barging in on a private matter.

Choosing each of our children's baby books was also an intimate experience. Since I was the one who would be the recorder of the events, I wanted to make sure that the book I bought for each of my daughters provided what I knew I wanted: lots of empty space to jot down thoughts

The Name Game: We Have a Winner

Having anointed me with a then-unique name, my parents could never find anything with the name "Leah" printed on it. I always longed for a "Leah" bicycle license plate, and since I could never find one, I swore I wouldn't subject my children to the same kind of frustration. I promised myself that I would give them simple names so that they would always be able to find stuff with their names on it. So, I christened my daughters Jane and Anne. But in this day and age, when Michaela and Catelyn are the names du jour, searching out items imprinted with "Jane" and "Anne" is about as fruitful as my search for Leah-imprinted items some thirty years ago.

That's why I was thrilled to learn about the NameTrain from Maple Landmark, a toy maker in Middlebury, Vermont. This charming wooden train features an engine and caboose, with the letters of your name in between. (I have the "Leah" version sitting in my office.) The festively colored letters are individual train cars, yielding an endless combination for today's modern names—or, in the case of my daughters, yesterday's classics. At about $30 (more for longer names), this train is just the ticket for babies as well as their older siblings. Maple Landmark also carries a variety of other wooden toys, which you can explore on the website at maplelandmark.com or by calling (800) 421-4223.

or put keepsakes, a calendar of momentous occasions, and a height and weight chart for tracking growth. Because I was so particular about what I wanted, it would have been almost impossible for someone to read my mind and buy this kind of book for me. Assuming that other parents will feel the same way, play it safe and leave it up to them to buy the right baby book for their needs.

Books for Baby

Some of the most meaningful moments I had in the days after my children were born were reading aloud to each child from the children's books that people had given us. Sure, my newborn was months away from bedtime stories when she could actually sit and look at the pictures, but I knew that reading to children, even at this tender age, could have long-term benefits.

I was raised in a home that teemed with books, and I knew from the very beginning that I wanted my children to grow up in the same kind of environment in which reading is revered. So, every book we received to commemorate the birth of our daughters was seen as a loving and thoughtful gift that would, we hoped, contribute to a lifelong love of reading. The books that meant the most were the ones that came with a personal inscription or card that described why the giver had chosen it. I discovered that some of my business colleagues had a softer side when it came to Hans Christian Andersen tales, and I was thrilled when

---

❧ The Best Gift I Ever Gave ❧

I recently attended my sister's baby shower. Her gift table was already overflowing with rattles, blankets, and bibs when she got to my gift—a camera. When she opened it and held it up, exclamations of "What a great gift!" and "Why didn't I think of that?" swept the room. I knew that new parents are avid picture-takers, so a camera—film or digital—would be a thoughtful gift that she could use for years to come.

Joanna, New York

> ### ⊰ *The Best Gift 1 Ever Got* ⊱
>
> My wife and I were in graduate school when our first child was born. Some friends gave my son and me matching Michigan sweatshirts for watching football games together. I was deeply touched by the gift—and amazed at how small his sweatshirt was compared with mine. I dressed him in that sweatshirt each week until his head got too big to fit inside the neck. Now a teddy bear in his room sports the sweatshirt.
>
> *Bill, Michigan*

friends shared how much their kids had enjoyed a certain Eric Carle book—and that they were giving it to one of my daughters in hopes that she would enjoy it as much.

I try to apply the same thinking when I'm buying a book for a child. If you have children, what are some of the books that they've enjoyed flipping through again and again? Are there certain books from your childhood that have withstood the test of time? These are good thoughts to keep in mind as you ponder which book to buy for a newborn. Most parents will be immensely pleased to add whatever book you settle on to the child's budding collection.

Clothing for Mother and Child

One of the fun things about being pregnant is acquiring an entirely new wardrobe—for yourself and your baby. In the early months of my pregnancies, I eagerly perused maternity shops for kicky leggings and comfy tops, but I must admit that by a certain stage in my pregnancy, I couldn't justify buying new clothes. Even though all of me was getting bigger, I knew that in a few months, I wouldn't need maternity clothes anymore, so I reasoned that I could live with the ten or so pieces I owned.

Maternity Wear for the Mother-to-Be

Many mothers-to-be, and fathers as well, adopt a certain frugality during the pregnancy—especially in light of the fact that expenses are sure to increase once the baby arrives. That's why a splendid gift for an expectant mother, particularly in the last months of pregnancy, is a special

---

Gift-Giving FAQ

Q: Do you give a present to someone who is having a second baby? And, if so, should you buy something of equal value to what you spent on the first kid?

A: You should send a gift each time someone with whom you're close has a baby— whether it's the second or seventh. It's really not fair to the child or the family to send a gift only to the firstborn. The birth (or adoption) of each child comes with a unique set of circumstances worth celebrating, so recognize the good news with a gift.

As far as how much to spend, you can use the gift you bought for the first child as a guideline, but don't jump through hoops. Even though I'm a gift-giving expert, I don't keep a log of what I gave to whom and how much I spent. If I sent a friend's baby a gift three years ago and now she's had another child, I'm not going to rummage through my old credit card bills to determine exactly how generous I was before. Instead, I'll use my best judgment to find an appropriate gift for that child—and I'll be sure to send along a small gift to the big brother or big sister as well.

---

item of maternity clothing or a gift certificate that she can use to take herself shopping.

About seven months into my first pregnancy, Bill and I traveled to San Francisco on a business trip for him and a brief vacation for us. Sure, I was excited about seeing the trolleys, the hilly streets, and the Golden Gate Bridge, but what I was really jazzed up about was the prospect of giving myself carte blanche to shop at the city's Japanese Weekend store. Japanese Weekend is a manufacturer of funky maternity clothes that has only a few retail outlets around the country. I'd read about these cool duds in my parenting books and magazines, but I'd never had the chance to try any of the stuff on because there were no stores near us. So, one morning when Bill had business to conduct, I made a beeline for Japanese Weekend, where I roamed among some of the most fashion-forward maternity clothes I'd ever laid eyes on. I returned triumphant with a pair of paisley-print overalls for myself and some shirts and accessories for a few of my pregnant pals back home, which they drooled over too.

Use the Internet

I recently discovered that had I been pregnant after the birth of on-line shopping, I wouldn't have had to schlep to San Francisco to get the Japanese Weekend clothes my friends and I crave. It turns out that the Internet is an almost effortless way to get your itchy hands on super maternity clothes, including certain items that aren't available in brick-and-mortar stores. Best of all, if you're shopping for a friend who lives far away, the Web retailer can wrap the gift for you, enclose a greeting, and deliver the package to your friend's doorstep. Here are two superb sites that I recommend you surf over to when you're in the market for maternity clothes for yourself or a special friend.

Target.com. Like the brick-and-mortar version, what's not to love about Target.com? The site claims to have more than 15,000 items on it—about right when you consider the wide variety of items in the stores. For a long-distance friend who is expecting, be sure to check out Target's darling "In Due Time" line of maternity wear (available on the website), and choose something that can be delivered directly to her. While the selection can be somewhat limited, the clothes are fashionable and functional and the prices are just right. Best of all, should your gift selection miss the mark, the recipient can return it, within 90 days and with the shipping receipt, to any of Target's more than 900 stores for a full refund.

GapMaternity. Ubiquitous retailer Gap has delved into the maternity world. On-line at GapMaternity, part of Gap.com, it's all expectant wear all the time. If mothers-to-be had their druthers (and unlimited funds alongside), they'd likely be pointing and clicking their way to a new expectant wardrobe compliments of GapMaternity. Here you'll find fashionable work staples, comfy casual clothes, and even items you'd expect

---

Gift Giving FYI

If you want a newborn to have a better chance of growing up a millionaire, give a gift of investing from the National Association of Investors Corporation (NAIC). For $20, plus a one-time $7 setup fee, you can sign a child up for NAIC membership and get a stock-investment program going. Call toll-free (877) ASK-NAIC (275-6242) or visit the better-investing.org website for the skinny.

---

to see at the Gap in your mall, such as boot-cut jeans, but these are made especially for a pregnant woman's expanding waistline. Just looking at these offerings makes me want to be pregnant again. That's why this website is a great place to shop when you want to present your pregnant friends with some new duds. And they'll appreciate that anything you buy them from the GapMaternity line that doesn't fit, or that they don't like, they can return to a regular Gap retail location or back to the website for free. (All orders come with a prepaid postage sticker.)

Clothes for Baby

When a friend or family member is expecting, it's always fun to go shopping for adorable outfits for the little tyke to come. Before I had kids, I delighted in having a reason to check out the children's department of my favorite store and in putting together an ensemble that I imagined would make a baby look like an angel. But then I had kids, and I started to look at children's clothing in a new way.

Clothes became something that you put on babies to keep them warm (or cool, depending on the season), and that was about it. When you needed to pack a diaper bag or grab an outfit in the morning—after not sleeping much the night before you weren't thinking about fashion but rather function. With countless diaper changes throughout the day, the best clothes were those that offered easy access (read: snaps on the legs). In addition, regardless of whether you were breast-feeding, bottle-feeding, or introducing solids, you were pretty much guaranteed that at least one meal of the day would end up somewhere on your baby's clothes. That meant a lot of dirty laundry and outfit changes. The best clothes were ones that weren't made of white fabric, didn't stain, could withstand multiple trips through the washer and dryer, and offered the aforementioned easy access.

Let me offer three examples of how seemingly adorable clothes that would seem to be the perfect new-baby gift are a nightmare in real life:

- That darling turtleneck-and-overalls outfit that makes the baby mannequin in the store look like a mini railroad engineer is actually a torture device for an infant. *You* try pulling a turtleneck over the head of a squirming baby and then changing a diaper under a pair of pants without snaps.

- That dress with the starched collar and stiff lace around the arms may as well be a straitjacket, since that's what it probably feels like to the baby who's wearing it. Also, long dresses are a bear to work with when you're buckling a child into a car seat.

- That gorgeous wool pea coat from the upscale Madison Avenue retailer may as well stay in the box forever. With its "dry clean only" label inside and the spit-up that's sure to land on it sometime during its first wearing, that coat is a goner for sure.

All of this doesn't mean that you shouldn't buy baby clothes as gifts. What you should do is keep the squirmy, fussy, wiggling nature of a baby and the hectic lives of the parents in mind when you shop. Following are my four S's for buying great baby clothes.

Stock Up on Staples

Beyond diapers, there are certain items that new parents can never have enough of. These include one-piece T-shirts that snap in the crotch so they stay tucked in, socks, legging-like pants that slide on and off easily, and hats (babies lose a lot of heat through their heads, so even during the summer, newborns usually have to keep their heads covered). Also, when you buy these, buy them in bulk. That way, the harried parents won't have those extra loads of laundry to do because Sweet Pea has soiled all of his T-shirts.

With shirts, aim for ones that snap down the front or along the shoulders—so the parents don't have to turn slipping a shirt over their baby's head into a flashback of the trip down the birth canal. I know firsthand that a baby is sure to freak out if darkness descends while you pull a shirt over its head. When my daughters were young, I learned to buy (and give as gifts) T-shirts from JC Penney that had an open front that snapped up the middle. There was no trauma involved when putting these on or taking them off.

Think Soft

If there's one thing that's going to make a bambino miserable (besides a dirty diaper, hunger, or sleepiness), it's uncomfortable clothes. Put your-

---

❦ The Best Gift I Ever Gave ❧

After we had the twins, I gave my husband a children's book called *Daddy and Me*. It's just pictures of babies and daddies doing different things together—shaving, jumping, tossing a ball, and so forth. Now, every night before they go to bed, he "reads" the twins this book and acts out what he sees in the pictures. It's so cute.

Leslie, New York

self in the baby's shoes—or pajamas, if you will. I'm definitely a happier person when I'm wearing a soft, comfortable outfit; why should a tyke be any different? When my children were babies, the clothes that we used over and over were those made of soft fabrics, such as terry-cloth footed pajamas and cotton jumpsuits. We also favored stretch fabrics, which came in handy as my kids became more mobile and began creeping along the floor.

Snaps Are a Must

I can't stress enough how important this easy-access thing is, and when it comes to baby clothes, snaps are the way to go. When you have a wailing child and need to get to a dirty diaper quickly, you don't want to fuss with buttons or ties. You want to be able to rip off the soiled clothes and whisk the baby into dry, clean clothes (and thereby put an end to the crying). Trusty snaps pretty much allow you to do that without ruining an outfit. Don't think that zippers will work as well: while they may offer the expediency element, I've known too many parents (myself included) who accidentally zipped their child's tender flesh when getting the baby dressed. So, when in doubt, go with snaps.

Size Up

Until you've had a baby of your own, you have no idea how quickly these little guys can grow. But grow they do. The average baby more than doubles its birth weight by the time it is six months old, and many do so long before the half-year mark. In fact, when they were only two months, both of my children weighed twice as much as they did when they were born. When you apply that phenomenon to buying clothes for a baby, you realize how ridiculous the newborn size is. Yes, it's usually perfect for a coming-home-from-the-hospital outfit, but a week later, that same

> ### ⚔ *The Best Gift I Ever Got* ⚔
>
> When I had my first baby, my coworkers sent me several trays of food,
> loaves of bread, and desserts from an Italian gourmet cafè near my home.
> I had enough eggplant parmigiana, stuffed manicotti, and baked ziti to eat
> and freeze for later. All told, that food gave us two weeks' worth of meals,
> which we really appreciated, since it took me extra long to get up and run-
> ning after my C-section.
>
> *Jennifer, Ohio*

outfit will probably be too snug. That's why I recommend that people
size up when shopping for clothes—and then some.

Let's say your friend had a bouncing baby boy in August. You just saw
the world's cutest cotton sleeper for Christmas and were planning on buying the four-to-six-months size. But don't. While the child will be four
months old when Saint Nick pays a visit, there's a good chance that he'll
be wearing six-months or bigger clothing. My rule of thumb is this: When
in doubt, buy a size bigger. Even when you know the height and weight
of the baby and can plot the numbers on a size chart in the store, you
should buy the next size up. This guarantees a longer wearing time, since
the baby can grow into the outfit, and it covers you if a manufacturer
tends to cut clothes on the smaller side, which many do, unfortunately.

Gifts for Religious Ceremonies

Religious ceremonies for newly born children are usually a way of welcoming them into a house of worship and the surrounding community.

If you are invited to a bris, a baby naming, or a baptism, it is customary to take a gift, even if you gave or sent something after the child was born. The pressure is compounded if you're one of the godparents.

Gifts for these kinds of ceremonies are usually classified very differently from other "birth" day gifts. In this case, toys are usually a no-no, and anything with a religious connotation is a yes-yes. A fine point to the rule is the silver christening cup, which godparents in the Christian religion tend to give their godchildren at the christening.

Here are some ideas on appropriate gifts to celebrate a newborn's religious service:

- Religious jewelry, such as a small Star of David or a cross—to be worn when the child is older

- An illustrated children's Bible or a Bible storybook

- For Jewish boys, a hand-knit or one-of-a-kind yarmulke (head covering)

- Donation to the child's house of worship or purchase of a dedicated item at that house of worship

- Art, decorative items, or prints of a religious or biblical nature (think anything Noah's Ark)

If you don't have a retail store nearby where you can find these kinds of items, try a museum store, either in person or on-line. MuseumShop.com, for example, offers gift-shop items from such institutions as the Vatican Library Collection, the Louvre, and the Israel Museum in Jerusalem.

> ### ❧ The Best Gift I Ever Got ❧
>
> When my daughter was born, one of my mother's friends sent a beautiful pillow made from vintage fabrics and ribbons in pale pink and white. It's monogrammed with my daughter's initials and is truly the centerpiece of her room. I hope she'll pass it on to her children someday.
>
> *Kathleen, Pennsylvania*

Keep Safety in Mind When Buying Toys

One transformation that usually occurs among parents after the baby is born is that they become the safety police—always on the lookout for dangers to their children. When my first daughter was born, there were news reports that certain kinds of window blinds emitted lead dust, and others posed a choking hazard. When we checked our windows, we discovered that we owned both of these kinds of blinds and promptly took them down.

What, you may be asking, do window blinds have to do with buying a baby gift? The answer is that they illustrate how something so seemingly innocuous could harm a child, and you wouldn't even know it. In my case, it was the blinds, something I'd purchased to decorate my home. For you, it could be that irresistible stuffed animal that you saw at the store, or a toy with small pieces that a baby could choke on. Stuffed animals and toys that have small pieces should be shunned from your list of possible baby gifts; they are better suited for older children.

The same goes for toys with long strings attached; the strings can wrap around a baby's neck.

For a heads-up about safe toys, including alerts to recalled toys, check out the website of the Consumer Products Safety Commission at cpsc.gov.

Don't Forget the Big Brother or Big Sister

When a baby is born, people sometimes forget that the child who was there before is also excited about having a new sibling and deserves a present to celebrate his or her new role in life as big brother or big sister. You don't need to go all out on a present for the older child; just make sure you get something. When you arrive to wish the new baby well, have a little wrapped present for any other children in the family to open and enjoy so they don't feel left out from all the excitement. Some fun gifts that my daughter Jane received when her sister Anne arrived were a pint-size apron and cooking utensils (so she could help Mommy and Daddy in the kitchen), and crayons and coloring books. They weren't big, but they meant a lot to her—and to us, too.

Baby Showers

Chances are if you know someone who is pregnant, you're going to be invited to a baby shower. These traditionally women-only gatherings usually feature a variety of silly games (such as identifying the baby food in an unlabeled jar) that would carry any modern woman back to her domestic roots. I've given and attended countless baby showers, and they are worlds apart from bridal showers.

A "Babyography"

Want to present a unique gift to a baby—a gift that is as one-of-a-kind as the child? Then, I direct you to the "Babyography" offered by the All About Baby company in Thousand Oaks, California. This eleven-by-fourteen-inch certificate provides a capsule of the day the child was born: in addition to the basic birth-certificate information, a "Babyography" includes fun facts about the child's birthday as well as trends during the year. Best of all, the certificate has whimsical illustrations such as alphabet blocks, a teddy bear, and a doll. It's perfect for framing and hanging in the nursery. For more information contact All About Baby at (800) 781-7171 or on-line at allbaby.com.

At a bridal shower, it's often the first time that both sides of the betrothed couple's family are socializing, which can make for some really awkward moments. By the time a baby shower rolls around, on the other hand, the principals have survived a wedding and probably a couple of holidays together, and everyone is more relaxed. And as far as baby shower gifts go, I say anything goes for the mother, the bundle of joy, and, if you want to cover all your bases, the father, too.

If you're lucky, the mother-to-be has registered (yes, you can do that now for events beyond weddings). If so, get thee a copy of her registry list, and go shopping for some of her must-have items. If you want to get a big-ticket purchase, suggest a few people chip in together. Obvious must-haves include car seats, strollers, baby carriers, and changing tables.

Even without a registry list to direct you, you can confidently pick out a great gift if you know the basics. One of the best gifts I ever received was a large Rubbermaid storage bin filled with diapers in a range of sizes, baby wipes, and diaper-rash cream. It probably didn't cost much money, but it was extremely thoughtful and practical. I put the contents to use the very day we came home from the hospital. And the bin came in handy for keeping baby clothes that my daughter outgrew and that I knew I'd eventually use with another child, which I did. Now, years later, that bin sits in my basement, storing off-season clothes. Talk about the gift that keeps on giving.

Other no-fail gifts include:

- *Baby clothes.* Just remember the four S's mentioned earlier.

- *Children's books.* Buying books that your own children enjoyed will make the gift more meaningful—especially if you tell the parents this in an inscription.

- *Bibs.* These are always helpful, and spitters—babies who spit up a lot—go through multiple bibs per day, so this gift is bound to get a workout.

- *Spill-proof "sippy" cups.* Many babies make the transition right from the breast or bottle to a sippy cup, so this will be a much-needed item a few months down the road.

- *CDs.* My cousin presented my husband and me with a Raffi CD after my first daughter was born, and a friend gave us a Peter, Paul, and Mary CD with "Puff, the Magic Dragon" on it. (That was one of my favorite songs as a child.) Those two recordings became the soundtrack of our life during those first few months as parents. I played them when I was rocking Jane to sleep, or Bill would put one on when we were just hanging out at home. Recently, Jane and her younger sister, Anne, discovered the Peter,

Paul, and Mary CD and asked to play it. We did, and now they know all the words to "Puff" just as I did at their age.

- *Picture frames and photo albums.* New parents take lots and lots of pictures of their bundle of joy. They'll definitely want to show off the photos of their adorable baby, and a picture frame or photo album lets them do it in style. Parents looking to splurge on a new-parent gift for their son or daughter, the new parent, may want to give a camera (video or still) as well.

- *Something for the expectant mother.* I know a woman who received a gift certificate to a spa for a pregnancy massage, followed by a manicure and pedicure, courtesy of her office colleagues. They told her that they assumed the remaining months of her pregnancy would be the last time she'd be able to indulge herself, so they wanted to help her do that. What fabulous, thoughtful friends this woman has.

Whatever you select to celebrate the new arrival, include a gift receipt for any purchase. That way, if for any reason the parents need to return the item, they'll know where you bought it (but not how much you spent), making the refund or exchange much easier for them.

~~ 3 ~~

ALL ABOUT ANNIVERSARIES

Every year, I find my wedding anniversary sneaking up on me, and before I know it, it's too late to buy my husband a gift. Fortunately, the same thing usually happens to him. So, a day or two before our anniversary, we'll usually ask if the other has got a gift, and since the answer is most likely no, we don't exchange gifts.

I realize that our non gift complacency probably seems like an awful tradition to have, but I have a confession: even though I'm a gift-giving expert, one gift-giving occasion that has always stumped me is anniversaries. Maybe it's because my parents divorced when I was young, so I never got into the habit of celebrating their anniversary. I now recognize that a chief reason I never thought to get my husband an anniversary gift is that I wasn't sure what kind of gift corresponds with which anniversary. For example, everyone knows that a couple married twenty-five years celebrates a silver anniversary, so an appropriate gift would be something silver. But my husband and I just marked our eighth anniversary. What do

---

Gift Giving FYI

A great resource for gifts containing some of the more unusual anniversary themes, such as willow and textiles, is the Berea College Crafts catalog and website (berea collegecrafts.com). The Kentucky college's crafts program, staffed with students and faculty, helps support the tuition-free status of this liberal arts school in the Appalachian region. The catalog and website are bursting with high-quality handmade crafts, including willow walking sticks ($15) and hand-woven table runners ($25) and placemats ($9 each), along with wood crafts, hand-blown glass objets d'art, and pottery.

---

you give on an eighth anniversary? Perhaps you're rusty on these gift-giving traditions, too.

Anniversary Gift Themes

I'm happy to report that you no longer have to be stymied—nor do I. In researching this chapter, I was able to pull together a comprehensive list of anniversary gift themes—both the classic and modern versions. On the next few pages, I'll tell you what these themes are, then offer appropriate gift suggestions. Now, while lesser shoppers may remain baffled about what to give for someone's eighth anniversary, as I was earlier this year, if you read on, you'll learn that looking to a gift of bronze, pottery, linens, or lace would be right on target.

A good catchall gift for any of the anniversary themes is a book that is related to the theme. Need a fourth-anniversary gift that involves flowers? Perhaps the couple would like to pore through a coffee-table book on annuals and perennials. For an eleventh-anniversary gift featuring steel, it won't be hard to produce a book about cars, a biography of Henry Ford, or, for the comic book lover, a compilation about the Man of Steel—Superman.

Before I get into specific suggestions, I should point out that there are certain five-year stretches of married life for which, as far as I can tell, no one has ever designated an appropriate gift theme. For example, you'll notice that my list skips from the fifteenth anniversary right to the twentieth. So, what do you do for anniversaries sixteen through nineteen? One option is to apply any of the general gift-giving advice packed in this book, such as the all-occasion appropriateness of housewares or gifts that reflect hobbies (especially ones the couple enjoys together).

In addition, for some reason, certain items appear as a theme more than once, such as wood, which is considered a classic gift for a fifth anniversary but a modern gift for a sixth anniversary. Similarly, leather is a classic gift for a third anniversary but a modern gift for the ninth. Rather than repeat myself throughout the chapter, I offer detailed gift ideas the first time a particular theme appears. Then later, when it appears again, I refer you back to my initial suggestions.

One timely tip on buying anniversary gifts for others is this: plan ahead, starting when they first get married. That is, when you're shopping for a wedding gift using a couple's registry list as your guide, don't throw that list away once you've made your purchase. It will come in handy years from now when you're searching for an appropriate anniversary gift. Since most retailers keep a registry list active only until a couple's first anniversary (some not even that long), you won't have access to it when you're searching for a fifth-anniversary gift. That's why it pays to plan ahead and keep that list on file.

First Anniversary

Classic: *Paper*   Modern: *Clocks*

Even though clocks are designated the modern first-anniversary gift, I think there's nothing more classic than a fine-quality timepiece. A husband could choose a watch with a fancy face for his wife, and the wife could give her husband a similarly nice watch or a decorative clock for his desk at work.

With the classic gift of paper, you have a full measure of options. You can stick to the straight and narrow and give a book or a gift certificate to a bookstore. Or you can order personalized stationery. A wife could give her husband notepaper with his monogram, or vice versa. More creative types can assemble a unique scrapbook of the couple's life together so far: this can include pictures from their dating days, or even earlier, notes of funny things they said as they were planning their wedding, souvenirs from the ceremony and reception such as matchbook covers or a copy of the invitation, and photographs from the honeymoon. Going in another direction, tickets to a concert also qualify as a gift of paper. Don't be afraid to have a little fun as you consider all the paper-related possibilities.

Second Anniversary

Classic: *Cotton*   Modern: *China*

The first thing that comes to mind when I think of cotton is something soft and wearable. Cotton flannel pajamas may warm the heart of that special someone to whom you've been married for two years; or, for a couple, you could try to find matching sets. You could also extend the sleep theme to include two-hundred-thread-count cotton pillowcases or a pretty cotton quilt.

Daytime clothing also fits the category. I would have been glad to receive a cotton twin sweater set for my second anniversary, and I'm sure my husband would have dug a cotton T-shirt from his alma mater.

If instead you go for the modern version of the second-anniversary gift, you can fill in the gaps in a couple's china pattern with a soup tureen or serving platter. Or, if you and your spouse never completed your china, you can buy each other a place setting — or suggest that family and friends do something similar when they ask what you'd like for your anniversary.

Third Anniversary

CLASSIC: *Leather*   MODERN: *Crystal or Glass*

I don't know about you, but I can never have enough crystal or cut glass to decorate my home and to hold flowers or use as serving pieces. Because of the nature of this modern third-anniversary gift, I think it's perfectly appropriate to go a little on the expensive side and seek out a top-quality manufacturer such as Waterford, Steuben, or Tiffany. Or, as with the second anniversary, you can refer to the recipient's gift registry list for a preference in stemware. Since pieces inevitably break or chip through wear and tear, supplying someone with an additional four crystal stems makes elegant sense.

With the gift of leather, the byword is conservative — avoid gag items or anything overtly sexual. In other words, stay away from chaps and leather teddies. Instead, you should focus on high-end stores that specializes in leather goods, such as Coach or Louis Vuitton — a world-class luggage and handbag maker. You usually can't go wrong with a leather belt, wallet, or business card holder.

Fourth Anniversary

Classic: *Fruit or Flowers*   Modern: *Electrical Appliance*

If you opt for the classic fourth-anniversary gift, you can get off pretty easy—whether it be for your spouse or someone else. Just send flowers or a gift basket of fruit, and you're done. If you go this route, choose a reputable vendor—one you've used previously and with whom you had a good experience, or a national company known for excellence. Two such companies that offer top-noch fruit and flowers are 1-800-FLOWERS and Harry and David.

As to modern gifts, you can get very small or very large. I mean, both a label maker and a refrigerator could be an appropriate electrical appliance for a fourth-anniversary gift, but they may seem a bit odd. A better bet is to buy an appliance that you know your spouse or the couple has been eyeing, such as a high-end coffeemaker or a cooking tool from the Food Network. If you're in the dark, you can always fall back on a gift certificate from a store that carries electrical appliances such as Staples or Lowe's, or a retailer of digital technology tools such as Sprint, AT&T Wireless, or Verizon.

Fifth Anniversary

Classic: *Wood*   Modern: *Silverware*

A quintessential wood-themed gift that represents the viability of a couple's marriage is a sapling to decorate their yard or a potted tree to keep inside. A couple celebrating their fifth anniversary during warm-weather months can plan to spend a day picking out a fruit-bearing or flowering tree at a local nursery and then planting it in their yard. Another avenue is to make the gift philanthropic: if the couple is of Jewish descent, have a tree planted in Israel; or donate to the National Arbor Day Foundation, which is responsible for planting nearly 450,000 trees across America and offers a Rain Forest Rescue program to help save trees abroad.

For a gift that doesn't need to be watered, you can limit yourself to something made from wood—a humidor for the guy who likes cigars, a mahogany jewelry box for the gal who never knows where to put her earrings and necklaces. Wooden birdhouses or picture frames are also low maintenance. And if you want to spring for something big, you can move up to a piece of wooden furniture.

The modern version of the fifth-anniversary gift—silverware—is pretty straightforward: all you've got to think about is buying forks, knives, and spoons. Ideally, they should match the couple's existing set. If it's a gift for each other, maybe you use this anniversary as an excuse to replace your mismatched silverware with a design you've always admired.

Sixth Anniversary

CLASSIC: *Candy or Iron*　MODERN: *Wood*

For a lead on non-run-of-the-mill gifts made from iron, look in your yellow pages for a local ironsmith whose shop you could visit. If there isn't a store near you, keep your eye out for craft fairs, where there's usually at least one ironsmith selling custom wares. In this category, I have a fondness for hanging pot racks, iron doorstops, and andirons for the fireplace.

The other classic sixth-anniversary gift is a hands-down favorite: candy. It's hard to find fault with a delicious box of sweets to celebrate being married six years. It's like Halloween, only better. Either a husband or wife could put together a big gift basket of the spouse's favorite treats.

Here's a more adventurous option: Go on a weekend trip with your spouse or friends to a nearby town where candy is made, and take a behind-the-scenes tour of the factory. You're guaranteed to get to sample lots of goodies. Best of all, most company factory tours are free. Here are two candy tours to consider:

Hershey Chocolate

In Hershey, Pennsylvania, the streets are practically paved with chocolate, since Hershey Foods is the dominating presence in this eponymous town near Harrisburg. You'll love the street lamps shaped like Hershey's Kisses, and if you're a chocoholic like me, you'll really love the simulated chocolate-making tour at the Hershey's Chocolate World Visitor's Center. At the end, you get free samples. Call (717) 534-4900 or click on the Chocolate World icon on the Hershey website at hersheys.com for more information.

For West Coasters, a Hershey factory tour is also available in the Golden State. It's at the company plant in Oakdale, California, where Hershey's Kisses are made. Call (209) 848-8126 for tour information.

Jelly Belly Jelly Beans

The Herman Goelitz company makes Jelly Belly jelly beans and Gummi candies in its Fairfield, California, plant outside Oakland. Visitors are welcome to tour the facility and taste freshly made jelly beans seven days a week. If you don't get enough to eat on the tour, the gift shop sells hundreds of varieties of yummy Gummis and delicious Jelly Belly prod-

---

ᴈ *The Best Gift 1 Ever Got* ᴇ

Now that we have kids, my husband and I have decided that it's silly to spend lots of money on anniversary gifts for each other. So, on our last anniversary, we got a sitter and just went out to dinner. After the meal, my husband started pulling out all these wrapped gifts, one after another. He'd broken our rule, and I felt bad that I didn't have anything for him. But then I started unwrapping the gifts, and inside each box was some of my favorite candy. One box had chocolates, another had candy corn, and then another had a large Peppermint Patty. It was a lot of fun to open the gifts and then eat them later. At least he hadn't spent a lot of money, as we'd originally agreed.

Leslie, New York

---

ucts, including two-pound bags of rejected (yet still good to eat) jelly beans called "Belly Flops." There's a similar factory and tour at the company's north Chicago location. On the Web visit jellybelly.com, or call (707) 428-2838 for the California factory or (847) 689-8950 for the Chicago factory.

For more great ideas on candy factories to tour for your sixth anniversary, look in a copy of *Watch It Made in the U.S.A.* (John Muir Publications, 1997) by Karen Axelrod and Bruce Brumberg, which describes nearly three hundred factory tours open to the public, from candy makers to car manufacturers.

For ideas on a modern sixth-anniversary gift made from wood, see the notes for the fifth anniversary.

Seventh Anniversary

CLASSIC: *Wool or Copper*   MODERN: *Desk Sets*

I have a relative who is a proficient knitter, and I'm always thrilled when she gives me a handmade wool sweater or throw. If you have a similar knack, and you need a seventh-anniversary gift, why not grab a ball of wool and knit one, purl two . . . ? Not only would it be appropriate for the anniversary, but it would also carry lasting sentiment, since you made it yourself. Of course, the same applies if you should happen to be a coppersmith. Make your favorite couple a stunning sculpture out of copper, and you'll be revered forever in their hearts.

Now, let's say you're restricted to more traditional means for producing a seventh-anniversary gift—say, the mall. No problem. Search out a pair of matching wool sweaters or a wool blanket. If you like the idea, look for decorative items made of copper, or functional but sleek pots or bowls at a cooking store.

For the modern version of the seventh-anniversary gift, I suggest a high-end pen set or coordinated desk accessories. In the latter case, you should know the decorating style of the office of the person or persons receiving the gift. You wouldn't want to present an op art desk set to someone whose office is done in a Shaker style.

Eighth Anniversary

CLASSIC: *Bronze or Pottery*   MODERN: *Linens or Lace*

With four themes to choose from, coming up with an eighth-anniversary gift should be a cinch. Since both bronze and pottery have artistic implications, a creative gift for spouses to give each other is enrollment in a workshop on bronze sculpture or pottery making at a local studio or community college. Or, if your schedules preclude that kind of time commitment, celebrate your anniversary by going out to dinner and then to a paint-your-own-pottery place, where you can spend the evening making each other a gift. This idea is also a great idea for children looking to give their parents an eighth-anniversary gift.

A luxurious gift from a husband to a wife involving linens and lace is a set of high-thread-count sheets (they're the softest) and some lace lingerie to go along with it. If you're buying for a couple, table linens and lace table accessories would do nicely, as would a gift certificate from a store where they can choose for themselves, such as Linens 'n Things.

Ninth Anniversary

CLASSIC: *Pottery or Willow*   MODERN: *Leather*

We've covered pottery (eighth) and leather (third), so you should already have some ideas to toss around for a ninth anniversary. That leaves us with willow. And I wonder if you had the same reaction that I did when I first discovered the concept of a willow gift: What the heck is that? Fear not, dear reader, I have an answer and a solution.

The willow gift, simply, must have something to do with a willow tree. There are all kinds of willows—weeping willows, corkscrew willows, and pussy willows (more a reed than a tree). So, willow-related gift options include planting a willow tree or buying the happily married couple a piece of furniture or a picture frame made of the trademark bent wood. I've seen decorative wreaths made of willow as well. The ultimately simple presentation of a bouquet of pussy willows tied with a pretty ribbon is another option.

Tenth Anniversary

CLASSIC: *Tin or Aluminum*   MODERN: *Diamond Jewelry*

For movie buffs who've been married ten years, videos of films with the word *tin* in the title would be a cool themed gift. These include *Pushing Tin*, *Tin Cup*, *Cat on a Hot Tin Roof*, and *Tin Men*. For collectors, you could search eBay or a local antiques fair for old-fashioned tin toys or lunchboxes.

Moving on to aluminum, instead of giving a gift of aluminum, how about using aluminum foil as gift wrap? For example, a husband could buy his wife a modern tenth-anniversary gift—diamond jewelry—and wrap the box in aluminum foil as a way to touch on the classic gift theme as well. If you're feeling a little zany and you're adept at folding aluminum foil into shapes, make the package look like a swan or some other figure, the way some restaurants do with doggy bags. Your beloved may be momentarily confused when presented with a gift that looks like leftover food, but that confusion will turn to delight when it reveals the diamond jewelry inside.

Eleventh Anniversary

CLASSIC: *Steel*   MODERN: *Jewelry*

When you think of steel, do you think of a cold, hard metal? Believe it or not, this metal can be the inspiration for terrific eleventh-anniversary gifts. Just consider the possibilities:

- Treat a football fan to a Pittsburgh Steelers game—whether they're the hometown team or the opponents.

- Hire a steel drum band to serenade your beloved with "your" song. Take this one step further and steal away to a Caribbean country for your anniversary, and listen to a homegrown steel drum band during your trip.

- Buy a set of high-end stainless steel cutlery or cookware.

- Present the handyman husband with a new set of tools made from steel.

- Get your spouse a new car.

With the jewelry theme of an eleventh-anniversary gift, your options are limitless—and admittedly skewed more to the wife than the husband. For a woman, you can't lose with earrings, a necklace, a bracelet, or a ring. For a man, you can present him with cuff links, a simple chain, or a new ring to match the wife's. If you've enjoyed traveling together, try to find a piece of jewelry, such as a pin, that represents where you've been.

Twelfth Anniversary

CLASSIC: *Silk or Linens*   MODERN: *Pearls*

While linen-related gifts should be fresh in your mind from the eighth-anniversary section, we've yet to touch on the subject of silk, a most glorious fabric. There are a number of wonderful silk gifts you and your spouse can get for each other or that you can give to a couple you know.

I think a marvelous gift that a husband can give to his wife and vice versa is silk underwear. Most guys really like how it feels to wear silk boxer shorts but probably can't justify buying a pair for themselves. Likewise, most women are drawn to the elegance of silk lingerie but see it as an indulgence. What better gift could there be than something you know the other will enjoy but would never buy on his or her own?

When you want something less intimate, you have a rainbow of choices with silk ties for him and silk scarves for her. Better yet, if business travel takes you to Asia, buy your silk gifts there. This region is known for its silk production, and your gift will mean all the more because it came from the other side of the world.

If you prefer pearls, the modern twelfth-anniversary gift, you can always buy her pearl jewelry. For him, look for items made with mother-of-pearl, such as a pocketknife, a watch fob, or cuff links.

Thirteenth Anniversary

CLASSIC: *Lace*   MODERN: *Textiles or Fur*

If you're not sure what qualifies as a textile gift, consider this: Webster's defines *textile* as cloth, especially woven or knit cloth. You could extrapolate this theme in a variety of ways: a hand-painted cloth tapestry for the home, an article of clothing, or a handmade quilt. You could even extend the meaning to include long-term benefits: stock in a textile company.

The other modern gift does have its pros and cons. Today's society doesn't look as kindly on fur as a fashion statement as it once did, so if you're not sure how the recipient will react to such a gift, escape the controversy with either the textile or lace theme. (For lace, go back to eighth anniversary.) However, if you're buying something for a woman who has been gushing that she'd love to own a fur coat or just a stole, then this anniversary would qualify as the time to fulfill that wish.

Coming down a step, you could always give fur with a collar—and a leash. If your family has been talking about getting a pet, use your thirteenth anniversary as your reason to finally add that dog, cat, hamster, or guinea pig to the household. Another option is to explore many types of fur—spend your anniversary at the zoo with the kids.

Fourteenth Anniversary

CLASSIC: *Ivory*   MODERN: *Gold Jewelry*

Because aqcuiring raw ivory usually involves killing elephants, I think it's best to eschew items actually made from ivory—assuming you can even find them. Many countries have banned them. That said, there's nothing wrong with giving a gift the color of ivory—such as a china vase. Or play on the theme with a gift related to pianos. "Tickling the ivories" can take the form of tickets to a piano concert or a CD of a famous pianist. Prime choices might be Billy Joel, Elton John, George Winston, or classical composer Debussy.

With gold jewelry, maybe this is the anniversary when you buy each other new gold wedding bands. Earrings, a bracelet, or a necklace would also make the grade.

Fifteenth Anniversary

CLASSIC: *Crystal*   MODERN: *Watch*

As with the first and third anniversaries, in regard to clocks and crystal, respectively, you can't go wrong with nice watches for you and your spouse or a decorative piece of cut crystal from a high-end company such as Tiffany or Waterford. A twist on the watch gift could be something involving Salvador Dali's well-known dripping watches: tickets to see a museum exhibit of his work, or a print or set of notepaper featuring this surreal image.

Twentieth Anniversary

CLASSIC: *China*   MODERN: *Platinum*

When the originators of anniversary gift themes chose china, I'm sure they were thinking of the kind you register for when you're getting married, but what would be even more wonderful is a trip to China. As with travel to any foreign country, going to China requires some preparation, especially since the Chinese government views personal rights differently from the way the American government does. Nonetheless, thousands of people travel to China regularly for business and pleasure and sing its praises. So, if it's an option, don't pass up the opportunity to create a memorable vacation.

If world-traveling isn't your cup of tea, choose the more sedate gift of something made of china. Or go with the modern version of the twentieth-anniversary gift, something made from platinum.

Platinum is considered one of the world's most resilient metals because it retains its sheen over time, and it complements precious gems in a way no other metal does. It's also very expensive, which is another reason it's so desirable. Any type of platinum gift would be overwhelmingly appreciated.

Silver Anniversary and Beyond

From this anniversary on, all of the themes revolve around precious metals or gemstones, making jewelry the most obvious gift between husbands and wives—perhaps earrings or a pin for her, cuff links or a ring for him. Furthermore, as you get up in years of marriage, classic and modern versions of designated anniversary gifts finally come together. So, if you're lucky enough to be married for a quarter century or more—

or if a couple close to you is—here are the classic and modern themes to help mark the occasion:

Anniversary	Classic	Modern
Twenty-Fifth	Silver	Silver
Thirtieth	Pearls	Diamond Jewelry
Thirty-Fifth	Coral	Jade
Fortieth	Ruby	Ruby
Forty-Fifth	Sapphire	Sapphire
Fiftieth	Gold	Gold
Fifty-Fifth	Emerald	Emerald
Sixtieth	Diamond	Diamond
Seventy-Fifth	Diamond (again)	Diamond (again)

✤ 4 ✤

BEST BETS FOR BIRTHDAYS

If our family's gift-giving decisions were left to my daughters, everyone would receive a Barbie doll for birthdays, Christmas, Chanukah, and all other gift-giving occasions. To them, the choice is as plain as the nose on their face: because *they* enjoy playing with Barbie dolls more than anything else in the whole world they naively reason that everyone else would love to receive one. And when we need to buy a birthday gift for one of their school friends, you can usually find us shopping in one of those very pink shopping aisles at the local toy store. While my daughters would love one of the ornate (and expensive) Barbie dolls, we generally confine our purchases to a couple of the more affordable models and maybe some Barbie furniture or clothes. I bet most other parents are like me: I want my children to be able to play with a gift with reckless abandon — and I don't want to worry that when Ken's head falls off, we've just tossed a ton of money down the toilet.

Quick Tips

To personalize your gift wrapping, invest in plain brown paper and a playful assortment of rubber stamps and ink pads. Then decorate the paper with images that relate to the gift-giving occasion or to the recipient's likes in general. For example, for a child who's intigrued by trains, planes, and automobiles, you can decorate with images of these modes of transportation. You can also adapt this type of decoration for other occasions, including Valentine's Day (hearts and flowers), Christmas and Chanukah (images of the season), and baby showers (anything in the nursery—booties, bottles, rattles).

❧ *The Best Gift I Ever Gave* ❧

Two years ago, I took time off to fly to Calgary to be with my brother on his fiftieth birthday. He didn't know I was coming. He answered the front door and burst into tears when he saw me standing there. I had a four-day visit, during which we skied, sang, and raised a glass (or two) to his fiftieth. The real gift, I believe, was the gift of time and my being able to be there to celebrate with him. I'm really close to my brother, but because we live so far apart, we don't get to see each other as much as we'd like. Since that first gift of time, my husband has done the same for his parents' birthdays, and recently we pooled our frequent-flier miles so that my husband's youngest sister could visit her parents and siblings on the West Coast for her fortieth birthday. What we've learned is that perhaps the most important gift on Earth is time spent with those we love.

Katharine, Quebec

✎ *The Best Gift 1 Ever Got* ✎

I'm a real outdoorsy type of person, so I was thrilled when I got an Appalachian Mountain Club membership as a birthday gift one year. What was cool was that my gift came packaged in a sports bottle along with the AMC magazine, *Outdoors*, and discount coupons to use on lodging and training. I've continued to renew my membership, and I go out and hike the White Mountains whenever I can.

Jim, Massachusetts

Finding the Perfect Birthday Gift

You wouldn't buy a grown-up a Barbie as a birthday gift—unless this adult happens to be a collector—but you can learn an important gift-giving lesson from my children: When you're not sure what to buy someone for a birthday, choose something that you enjoy yourself.

I don't mean to suggest that you give a meat-of-the-month-club membership to your sister who is an avowed vegetarian, but if you're at a loss for a gift, think back to some of the things you've enjoyed—and that would likely please the recipient in the same way. For example (and I know this sounds cliché), have you read any good books lately? Heard an awesome CD? Sipped a wine that was just superb? These are the kinds of questions you need to ask yourself as you contemplate prospective gifts.

In addition, as I mentioned earlier in the book, knowing the recipient's hobbies or pastimes can help clue you in on the optimum choice.

For example, my mother is a bird-watching fan like no other I've ever met. She keeps a pair of binoculars and a guide to North American birds on her kitchen table (and did when I was growing up) so that whenever she spots an interesting feathered friend in the trees, she can watch it then look it up in her book. Naturally enough, I often buy her bird-related gifts for her birthday. One year, we bought her some beautiful bird notepaper from the Metropolitan Museum of Art store. Another year, we had some fun and got a T-shirt from the Signals catalog illustrated with the bird poop markings of various species. Not long ago, at my local Lenox store, I spied a set of cake plates with a North American birds motif, and they are at the top of this year's idea list for Mom.

A challenge in giving birthday gifts to people you've known for a long time is that your gift ideas should change, albeit slightly, as the recipient gets older. While your nephew might have loved his annual Play-Doh

---

❧ The Best Gift I Ever Gave ❧

One year, I was stumped as to what to give my husband for his birthday, and I recalled how much he'd talked about a trip he'd taken to Cameroon years ago. It just so happened that a Museum of African Art had recently opened in our town, so I bought him a membership. Over the years, I've renewed the membership, and we've enjoyed going for members-only events. Just yesterday, he commented to me how much he appreciates the museum and how membership was a perfect gift for him.

Carol, New York

~❧ The Best Gift I Ever Gave ❧~

For my mother's sixtieth birthday, my sister and I put together a memory book of my mother's life. We sent out a page to friends, family members, coworkers, and the like and asked them to write something special that they remembered about my mother. We also requested that they attach a picture of themselves, ideally one with my mother in it. People offered great things—some poems, some just photos. It not only gave my sister and me additional insight into our mother's life, but it also reminded us how many people she'd touched. My mother was equally touched when she received it. Now that memory book has a special place in my life, since my mother died a few years ago, and it's a great way for me to remember her and what a great lady she was.

Jeanne, New York

Quick Tips

Does your gift recipient have a favorite local store—especially an eatery or a food shop? If so, why not buy him or her a gift package or certificate from that business? For example, we have a close friend who loves our small town's French bakery, whose owners moved from Paris and brought with them all of their pastry-making know-how. For his birthday last year, we bought him a gift certificate from this bakery so he could indulge in croissants and cakes to his heart's delight. Someone else I know sent a New Yorker–cum–Los Angelino a box of bagels from the transplant's beloved Manhattan bagel shop as a birthday gift one year. The gift was devoured in a New York minute.

loot for birthdays throughout elementary school, he'll probably think you are weird and outdated if you continue this tradition into his double-digit years. That's why this chapter neatly lays out birthday gift ideas for children, teenagers (for me, the most fickle and difficult group to buy for), and grown-ups—including grandparents. You'll even solve the riddle of what to give your childhood friends' children whom you do not know well.

Gifts for Children

It's just so easy to buy kids clothes as a birthday gift—especially infants, toddlers, and young children. You step into babyGap or Gymboree, and

---

Gift Giving FYI

How old is the birthday party? The Lenox Gift Company, maker of china and porcelain collectibles, did some checking. Here's a look at its collection of birthday facts:

- The first birthday celebration on record happened around 3000 B.C. Only high-ranking officials, such as Egyptian pharaohs, kings, queens, and noblemen, celebrated their birthdays.

- With the rise of Christianity, birthday celebrations ceased. However, once the world starting celebrating Christmas (the birth of Christ) in the fourth century, birthday celebrations for everyone began anew.

- The birthday party that we know of today actually began in thirteenth-century Germany and was called "Kinderfeste," or a celebration for young children. It involved a birthday cake with candles that stayed lit all day, gifts for the birthday boy or girl, and serving that child's favorite meal.

❧ *The Best Gift I Ever Got* ❧

For my fiftieth birthday, my wife sent me to the Richard Petty Driving Experience. I'm a real NASCAR fanatic, as is my wife, so this was a really cool gift. Here's how it works: I got about one hour of instruction, and then I got to drive an actual Winston Cup car around the track at Richmond (Va.) International Raceway for eight laps. My fastest lap was 106 mph. For a race fan, driving a real race car on a real NASCAR track is a dream come true!

Hank, Virginia

---

the outfit selections are so fetching that you want to buy out the store. I know. I've been there and done that, and I've learned that, while giving a cute outfit can work as *part* of a gift, it shouldn't be all that you give. Here's why: The next time you're invited to a children's birthday party, watch the collective reaction when the child opens a gift with clothes in it. The adults will probably ooh and aah, accompanied by a groupwide groan from the children. To a kid, there is nothing fun about getting clothing as a gift. To a kid, toys rule, and they should always be your first choice.

There is a notable exception to this rule, though: dress-up clothes do not count as regular clothing and can be purchased without reservation for any child who shows an affinity for this kind of pretend play. Likewise, an athletic uniform or shirt emblazoned with the number of the child's favorite sport star will most likely count as cool clothing.

So, what toys are good for kids? Here are some general rules:

- With babies, give a child-safe toy (read the label or box for indi-
cations) that the infant can grip and that makes noise. A wiggle
worm with a rattle in its tail was one of my children's early
favorites.

- Toddlers and preschoolers love to use their bodies, so anything that
gives them freedom to run, push, or build something is key. Stack-
ing cups, a pretend lawn mower, or a child-size baby carriage for
taking their dolls on a walk will be used and loved.

- Children of elementary school age have more sophisticated taste
in toys and tend to favor games, either board or electronic. One
that I fondly remember and that is now among my kindergartner's
top picks is Chutes and Ladders, an exceptionally simple board

---

❧ The Best Gift I Ever Gave ❧

I have an eighty-nine-year-old widowed mother who still lives alone, is rea-
sonably active, doesn't drive, and has everything she needs. She tells us
each year that she wants nothing. Last year, we came up with a creative
solution. My siblings and I, along with our fourteen grown children and
their sixteen children, sent her eighty-nine black-eyed Susans for her birthday, followed by two living black-eyed Susan plants that she could enjoy
all summer long. By the way, my mother's name is Susan, so the flowers
had a special significance to her. We're planning to send her ninety roses
next year, since roses are her favorite flower.

Carol, Florida

❧ *The Best Gift I Ever Got* ❧

When I turned sixteen, my birthday present from my mother was a certificate for an introductory flight lesson. That one lesson opened up the world of aviation to me. I went on to get my commercial, instrument, and multiengine ratings and continue to fly today—some thirty years later.

Betsy, Florida

---

game. Another perennial pick is Candy Land. If you're unsure what a ten-year-old would like to receive, ask one. When you're roaming through a store such as Target or Toys R Us looking for a present, stop parents with a child in tow who looks about the age of your gift recipient and ask what that child likes to play with. This informal polling of your target audience should point you in the right direction.

Gifts for Teenagers

These young adults are a tough crowd to please. They are so tuned in to the latest fads and crazes that a totally cool gift you buy in March for an April birthday may be old news by the time the party rolls around. That's why I believe your best bet when buying for teenagers is a gift certificate from a bricks-and-mortar or on-line store where you know they'll find something they like. Good places to consider include Target, Tower Records, and Blockbuster video stores, all of which sell gift cards in a variety of denominations.

> ### ❧ *The Best Gift I Ever Gave* ❧
>
> For my boyfriend's birthday, I bought him a hiking backpack to match the
> one I used whenever we went backpacking. This pack has ten pockets, and
> I filled each of them with a different gift. In one, I put a CD that he wanted;
> in another, a printout of three super-8 cameras I'd ordered for him on eBay.
> There was also a guidebook to Cuba, since we were going there in a week.
> Each time he found another gift in the pocket, he was shocked and more
> grateful. I continued the tradition the next year with a new bag, but this
> time, I put in each pocket something he'd lost over the past year (but that
> I found or repurchased for him). The stuff included his favorite Gap base-
> ball hat and a new wallet.
>
> *Heidi, New York*

Here's one reason I believe this approach works best with teenagers.
I have a teenage half brother whom I don't see often, so I don't know his
likes and dislikes very well. When I give him a birthday gift, I want it to
be something he'll use and enjoy. A few years ago, I decided on a $25 gift
certificate to Amazon.com, which elicited the most enthusiastic thank-
you note I'd ever received from a relative, let alone a teen. So, the next
birthday, I repeated the gift. This past summer, I happened to see my half
brother shortly before his birthday and told him that I wasn't sure if he'd
want to get the Amazon.com gift certificate yet again. "Are you kid-
ding?" he said. "I love that gift. It's the best." Based on that response, I'll
probably continue to buy him that gift certificate until he's in his twen-

ties — or until I ask him again in a few years and he gives me a different response.

Gifts for Adults

Once we reach our adult years, it becomes harder and harder to justify giving each other more "stuff." I speak as a home owner whose garage and basement are both overflowing with "stuff." That's why it's important to target your adult gift-giving toward something you're confident the recipient will like and use. Case in point: the bird-related gifts I tend to give my mother, because I know that bird-watching continues to be one of her hobbies.

Here's another example of how hobbies can tell you a lot about potential gifts for someone. A woman I know has a sister who is an obsessed

---

➤ The Best Gift I Ever Got ➤

I've always loved giraffes. For my forty-fifth birthday, my husband asked me to meet him for lunch—and at the zoo, of all places. I was a little surprised but open to the possibilities. It turned out that he'd arranged for me to have a private audience with the zoo's giraffe. I got to stand right next to the giraffe, pat it, and feed it bananas. (You have no idea how long a giraffe's tongue is until you get up close and personal.) My husband took a picture of the giraffe and me, and I treasure that picture—as well as that birthday gift.

Carolyn, Ohio

~ The Best Gift I Ever Gave ~

Before we were married, my husband, Todd, was living in Texas, and I was living in New Jersey. Every time I talked to him, he raved about an Austin restaurant called The Salt Lick, which makes out-of-this-world barbeque. Years later, I discovered that The Salt Lick had opened a mail-order business. With Todd's birthday around the corner (he was with me in New Jersey by now), I decided to order him dinner from The Salt Lick as his gift. It arrived on his birthday in a cooler of dry ice, and he told me it was the best and most unexpected gift he'd ever received. This one package of food ended up giving us ten delicious dinners.

Jeannine, California

garage sale–goer. She's a creative person who knows how to turn other people's castoffs into personal treasures. Each weekend, she's out scouting her local area for sales. For a few birthdays running, my friend has given her sister something that she could use on her treks. One year, it was a laminated, spiral-bound atlas of her area, since the foldout map she'd been using was worn out and starting to tear. The next year, she bought a nifty spill-proof travel mug so her sister could get her caffeine fix in transit and not have to worry about spilling her coffee all over the place. The bargain hunter has used each of these gifts with enthusiasm, because the giver chose them to complement her passion.

Of course, not every person to whom you'll be giving a birthday gift is obvious about his or her likes, dislikes, and hobbies. That's why a gift certificate from a retailer along the lines of Target or Amazon.com, where there's something for everyone, should do in a pinch.

Overall, the most challenging adults to buy for are parents or grandparents. My first line of defense is always to ask the person what he or she would like. However, I realize that parents can sometimes give you an answer like "Oh, honey, I don't need anything. I have everything I'd ever want," which can send you screaming to the shrink—not to mention throw a wrench into your gift-buying works. But don't let this response lead you to avoid gift giving altogether. I believe that you must always remember your parents or grandparents on their birthdays, even if it's just with a bouquet of flowers delivered from the local florist. For more pizzazz, buy them something that they would never get for themselves—an expensive bottle of wine that your dad can use to toast his birthday or a gift certificate from a local nail salon so that your grandmother can treat herself to a pedicure.

Of course, an all-time favorite gift for parents and grandparents is a nicely framed photograph of you or, even better if you have them, your kids. I've yet to see a parent or grandparent who didn't wax sentimental when presented with a picture of their offspring or their offspring's offspring. You can expand the photo idea a bit and do a picture of you and the kids on a mug or sweatshirt. Grandparents love this kind of stuff.

~<e 5 ~>

THE BUSINESS OF GIVING BUSINESS GIFTS

I learned firsthand what makes an outstanding business gift many years ago when I was working as an assistant at a magazine in New York City. I worked for two executives, and that first holiday, they both gave me gifts that went above and beyond the ordinary. One was a silver-plated pen from Tiffany, and the other was a gift certificate for a half day at Georgette Klinger, an upscale spa. Those gifts were so timeless and classic that even though I received them more than a decade ago, I'd give either of them in a second to a colleague or employee today.

What makes a pen and a gift certificate so extraordinary? First, the pen was from the venerable institution Tiffany & Company. It was a beautiful pen, and I thought of my boss's generosity each time I used it to sign his correspondence and my own. But what made the gift so memorable is what happened when he handed it to me. It was the first time anyone had ever given me anything from Tiffany, so receiving the trademark robin's egg blue box tied with a satiny white ribbon literally made me gasp, and I broke into a broad smile. It didn't matter to me what was inside; I was just so pleased that someone had bought me something from Tiffany. I've since received many gifts from Tiffany, and I still get excited each time someone gives me one of those gorgeous blue boxes.

The gift certificate meant a lot for a different reason. My boss recognized that as a young person just out of college, I couldn't afford to pamper myself with spa treatments. She knew that a little indulgence

---

Small Business Gifts

Corporate gift giving isn't for big businesses only. Plenty of entrepreneurs and owners of small businesses engage in a gift exchange at the holidays. Here are some statistics from a recent American Express Small Business Gift-Buying Survey:

- More than three million small business owners buy corporate gifts each year, spending on average about $1,800 for these gifts.
- Employees are the most often cited recipients, followed by clients and vendors.
- The best way to make sure your employees and clients enjoy your gift? Feed them. Food is one of the most popular gifts. Money and, believe it or not, office supplies are perennial favorites as well.
- Gift giving isn't just being nice; it's good business. Of the owners surveyed, 78 percent said that holiday gift giving has helped to improve business; 71 percent said that gift giving is an important part of the company's marketing plan; and 84 percent reported that giving employees a holiday gift helped to boost morale.

> ### ~✖ The Best Gift I Ever Gave ✖~
>
> In the past, I've puzzled about a good gift to give clients. I knew I wanted to give some sort of gift basket, but I wasn't sure which kind. Then I discovered Wolferman's, a Kansas company that is known for its gourmet English muffins, scones, marmalade, coffees, and teas. I love sending them because they are distinctive and because I feel as if I'm treating the office to a morning coffee break.
>
> *Margie, Massachusetts*

now and again could do wonders for a person's outlook as well as her appearance. In addition, she knew that I looked up to her as a mentor, and I believe she chose this spa because she went there herself. Not only could she vouch for the quality of the services, but also it was her way of letting me feel just like her for a few hours. After Christmas, I made an appointment for a facial, manicure, and pedicure (my first all-around), and when I walked out of the spa, I was on cloud nine.

That year, I wrote two of the most heartfelt thank-you notes of my professional career.

Best Bets for Business Gifts

So, now you know that I like packages from Tiffany and gift certificates for pampering. While the examples I've cited were holiday gifts, the rules for what's appropriate to give in a business setting apply for all gift-giving occasions—birthdays, promotions, or the birth or adoption of a child. Here are some ideas to keep in mind as you make your corporate gift-giving decisions.

Buy from Upscale Retailers

One more time: as far as I'm concerned, anything that comes in a blue Tiffany box is money well spent. That's because the value of a gift from Tiffany is magnified by the experience of opening it. The same can be said for gifts from other well-known institutions that have either familiar packaging (think gold box from Godiva) or a name that people automatically associate with high quality, such as Saks Fifth Avenue, Neiman-Marcus, or Crate & Barrel. Also worthy of this category: a boutique in your town that everyone recognizes as top of the line.

Treat Someone to a Service

Because I could never have afforded to splurge on a spa treatment for myself, my boss's gift meant that much more to me. Years later, I gave a gift certificate for a manicure to each of the women who worked at the day care center that my daughters attended. Think first of anything pampering-related when you want a wonderful gift for support staff. Another possibility is gift certificates from restaurants in your area where you've eaten and you're confident your secretary or office mate would enjoy having a meal. Or, if you know that your client or colleague frequents a specific spa, buy a gift certificate for a treatment there.

Food Has Mass Appeal

Currently, the gift I give all of my corporate clients is a box of chocolate truffles from Harry and David. I reason that most people would never buy themselves a box of chocolates to indulge in, so I do it for them. The

Celebrity Gifts

While we think of award shows, such as the Emmys and the Academy Awards, as ways of rewarding actors for their work, the entertainers who present the statues are rewarded themselves with the ultimate corporate gift: each year, presenters at these ceremonies get an enormous gift basket as a thank-you for participating. According to *US Weekly* magazine, presenters at the 2000 Emmy Awards went home with more than $8,000 worth of merchandise. Some of the more notable loot (much of which I wish someone would bestow on *me*) and its value includes:

- Gift certificate for a reflexology session and sea-salt pedicure at Frederic Fekkai ($75)
- Razor scooter from Sharper Image ($100)
- MAC cosmetics ($500)
- A bottle each of Absolut Currant vodka ($20) and Piper-Heidsieck champagne ($40)
- Sonicare electric toothbrush ($110)
- $50 American Express gift cheque
- Nokia cell phone ($800)
  Large Longaberger basket ($325)

main appeal of giving chocolates is that they're appropriate across the corporate spectrum—from your company's receptionist to the president and CEO.

Also in this category are fruit baskets and sweet treats, such as cookies and brownies. The bonus to giving food is that the recipient can share the gift with coworkers or family, which lets you both spread the cheer. Of course, if the person avoids certain foods because of health or

---

~ The Best Gift 1 Ever Got ~

A client of mine sent me a box of chocolate truffles for Christmas one year, which arrived on the same day that we found out there would likely be layoffs in the near future. That box of chocolates was the perfect pick-me-up for a very gloomy day at the office.

Kay, California

---

religious reasons, you'll need to take that into account. For example, I have one client with diabetes, so instead of sending food, I send flowers.

Greenery Is Good

A universal gift for a client or staff member is a bouquet of fresh-cut flowers. I don't know a soul who doesn't brighten at the receipt of fresh blooms. If a bouquet would convey the wrong sentiment, order up a more conservative potted plant; for holidays, these would include seasonal flowers such as a poinsettia or Christmas cactus, or a lily for Easter.

Stay Within Bounds

Generally speaking, there's nothing wrong with giving a personalized business gift that pertains to the recipient's hobby. For example, I know a businessperson who gave a horseback riding–loving client a coffee-table book on Thoroughbreds. However, you have to tread carefully when you enter this territory. Why? Because some seemingly utilitarian gifts may violate a company policy and cause the recipient trouble. A case in point is a company that strictly forbids alcohol on the premises:

while a bottle of wine may seem like a good choice for a collector, under these circumstances it could blow up in your face—or the recipient's. Also avoid any gifts that could be interpreted as sexual in any respect. You don't want a holiday or birthday gift to result in your getting slapped with a sexual harassment suit. Lingerie may seem like the ideal gift for a woman associate, but even a gift certificate to a lingerie store—no matter how much the person may like it—can have the wrong connotations. Don't give anyone the slightest reason to misinterpret your message.

Gifts Going to Other Countries

With today's global economy, you may well have to send a gift to a business colleague or client in another country. While the gift-giving rules in English-speaking countries such as Canada, the United Kingdom, and Australia tend to resemble those in the United States, the customs in some other places around the globe could render your well-meaning gift an insult or, worse, a death wish. I recently spoke with Sheida Hodge at Berlitz International in Princeton, New Jersey, who specializes in training foreign-bound executives on what they need to know about the local culture and customs, including gift giving. Following are some of her pointers on giving gifts to an international clientele.

Colors Have Certain Connotations

You might have noticed that Asian brides wear bright red wedding dresses, but did you know why? White is considered the color of death in Asian countries such as China, Korea, and Vietnam, thus the colorful wedding attire. Black has the same connotation, and that's why, regardless of what you buy an Asian business associate, you should never present it in a black-and-white box. Red is the color of happiness and is always a good choice for gift packaging, if not for the gift itself.

There are a number of other ways a certain color can trip you up. For example, in the United States, sending someone yellow roses signifies friendship, but in certain European countries, including France, Spain, and Germany, yellow roses mean anything but friendship. In France, for instance, yellow is the color of infidelity. In Spain, yellow and white flowers are sent when someone dies.

Timepieces Are Taboo

Like the color white, for many Asians timepieces such as clocks and watches have a death connotation—perhaps precisely because they show the passing of time. While Asians have clocks in their homes and offices, and they wear watches just as Americans do, to give a timepiece as a gift is not appropriate.

Knives of Any Kind Can Give Offense

To an American, a letter opener is a benign corporate gift. To a person of Asian descent, this is not so. The same caveat holds for a set of knives as a wedding gift for a business associate. That's because knives and other cutting instruments often represent tools of suicide in Asian communities. People in Latin America and the Middle East may attach similar meanings to knives, so ban anything bladed from your business gift list.

Go for Substance

Regardless of how much you spend on a business gift, if it doesn't seem substantial, it won't be well received by a client overseas. People in Europe, Asia, Latin America, and elsewhere tend to be very status-conscious—even more so than Americans—so a gift from a company

---

⚜ The Best Gift 1 Ever Got ⚜

When I was a fashion editor in New York, I was always getting flowers and wine as gifts. One year, a public relations person with whom I'd worked sent me three current books on fashion, all of them coffee-table style. It was a unique gift that I enjoyed so much that I actually read each from cover to cover.

Kathleen, Pennsylvania

---

with a recognizable and revered name, such as Tiffany or Godiva, is always welcomed. If you're going to give a pen, for instance, you'll make the strongest impression if it's from a well-known manufacturer such as Montblanc or Waterman.

Read Labels

Let's say you're congratulating yourself on finding the just-right gift for your colleague in China. It's from a well-known store, and it seems to be good quality, but when you happen to turn it over and read the label, you see that it was made somewhere other than the United States. What should you do? Take it back. People around the globe are often more label-conscious than Americans and don't want to receive a gift that was made in their own backyard or, worse, a place where merchandise is mass-produced. To maintain goodwill, you're wise to buy items that are made in the U.S.A. or other countries with special appeal, such as Ireland for crystal or France for wine.

If you can't tell where a gift you're considering buying was made, ask. If the salesperson doesn't give you a satisfactory answer, shop elsewhere.

If you want to remove the uncertainty from your shopping, do business with retailers that understand the importance of identifying a product's origin. For example, the L.L.Bean corporate sales catalog specifies which products are made in America (sometimes denoting if a product was made right in New England, where the company is headquartered) and which are imported.

Chocolates Are (Almost) Always a Good Choice

If there's one gift that is globally accepted, it's boxed chocolates—for many of the reasons previously mentioned. They're an indulgence that most people wouldn't buy for themselves, they're a taste treat, and they can be shared with family or colleagues. In addition, many varieties bear the stamp of an upscale retailer and are American-made products. However, there is a wrinkle in chocolate's perfection: don't send them to people in countries known for their own chocolate industry, such as Switzerland, Belgium, and France.

The Key to Key Chains

Since businesspeople worldwide carry keys—to their homes, offices, cars, even computers—key chains are always a safe gift. Give it distinction by purchasing the accessory from a store with distinction, such as Tiffany, so that the item will seem substantial to the recipient.

Go With Upscale Liquors

Unlike in the American workplace, liquor isn't such a taboo in many offices overseas. If you'd like to send some spirits—either distilled or fermented—to one of those offices, do it with class by selecting a top-shelf brand such as Chivas Regal or Glenlivet. Or send a local product distinct to your area of the country. For example, if you're based in the Silicon Valley and you want to send a bottle of wine to a foreign colleague, choose one from a vineyard in Napa or Sonoma.

Consider the Client's Culture

While an upscale liquor would be eminently suitable for a typical Japanese client, it would be objectionable to another client elsewhere in Asia—specifically in Islamic countries where alcohol is a no-no. You face another prohibition in countries where the Hindu religion prevails: anything that is made from leather is a sacrilege, since cows are holy to Hindus. To add to that, for many Asians, certain numerical combinations represent bad luck. Anything in groups of four is verboten. So, if you're going to give serving pieces such as glasses or coasters, don't give sets of four, eight, or twelve, as is the custom in the United States. Instead, go with five. As for glassware, the Asian culture holds anything having to do with light as being good, so a cut crystal vase or a mirror is a good choice.

Brush Up on International Etiquette

If your travel schedule allows, you may want to present the gift to your foreign colleague in person. Get off on the right foot by minding these rules of etiquette:

Watch Your Hands

In many Asian countries, it is polite to pass an object to someone with both hands. In an Islamic country, use only your right; using the left hand is bad manners because it is associated with tending to one's personal hygiene. Also, often a male presenting a gift to a female, or vice versa, should not touch the woman, let alone kiss her on the cheek, dur-

---

Charitable Gifts

Making a donation to a good cause can be a worthy business gift. I know a business owner who finds out what charitable organizations her clients support, and then at holiday time, she makes a donation in the client's name. When she sends a holiday card, she encloses a note letting the person know of the contribution she's made in lieu of a traditional holiday gift.

---

ing the presentation, since the religion or culture may prohibit any physical exchange between people of the opposite sex who are not married to each other.

Refusal Is Acceptance

If you were to offer a gift to an American and the person refused to accept it, you'd probably utter "Oh, OK" and put the gift away. But in some foreign cultures, refusing a gift is actually a way of being polite. So, if you present a gift to someone and are rebuffed, offer it again. Let the person know that it was no trouble to buy this gift (even if it was), and persist until you're successful. It may take a couple of times back and forth of you offering and the would-be recipient refusing, but this is just part of being polite in certain cultures.

Gifts Are Opened in Privacy

Another surprise to many Americans is that in some cultures, people don't open gifts in front of the giver. If you present a gift to someone who puts it away unopened, accept that this is the way things are done and that the recipient is just being polite, according to local custom. Likewise, if your gift does not elicit a gush of thank-yous, don't be dismayed. In many cultures, it is rude to thank a gift giver repeatedly.

~ 6 ~

HOW-TOS FOR THE
HOLIDAY SEASON

It's easy for me to get in a gift-giving mood at holiday time. Unbridled commercialism notwithstanding, it's a time to show people that you care for them. While the holidays can be exhausting, the look on a friend's face when he or she pulls open that bow makes all the work and stress of shopping worth it. Even though I'm an expert on this, I don't give what would be considered extravagant gifts Instead, I've become a pro at zeroing in on things that people really want or will really use, which is the secret of gift-giving cheer.

Holiday Gift-Planning Tips

This past Christmas, we gave our neighbors poinsettias—a common holiday token—but I was able to turn a conventional gift into one that was unique and affordable and that truly conveyed a message of caring.

Here's what I did—and what you can do, too, when planning holiday gift-giving to neighbors and friends.

Plan Ahead

I ordered the poinsettias from my daughters' school in October, when most people were thinking Halloween, not Christmas. The school was running a poinsettia fund-raiser that promised not only attractive prices but also plants in a variety of color combinations that you couldn't find at the local florist. We ordered some plants with peppermint-striped leaves, some with leaves the color of pink cotton candy, as well as cherry

---

✤ The Best Gift I Ever Gave ✤

The best gift I ever gave my parents was one of the simplest: a calendar you get at a quick-copy place that has a different photo that you provide for each month of the year. I dug way back into pictures from my childhood and enlisted my sister's help in finding the most meaningful images to match each month. For example, for the month of my parents' wedding anniversary, I used a shot of them on their wedding day. For December, I selected a really neat family photo in front of the Christmas tree from thirty years ago. Tears welled in their eyes as they flipped through the pages and recalled all those memories. That was years ago, and my mother still has that calendar on her refrigerator; she turns the page each month for the sake of the picture, not the calendar itself.

Therese, California

❧ The Best Gift 1 Ever Gave ❧

When our daughter was five, she had to have heart surgery in mid-December. In the hospital, she asked Santa to bring her a playhouse for Christmas. She'd been through so much that we were determined to make her wish come true, so we arranged to have a playhouse built in our backyard in time for Christmas. The look on her face on Christmas morning, when she came home from the hospital, was worth every penny we spent on the playhouse.

Miriam, California

---

red and snow white ones. All told, I probably spent $50. The plants arrived in early December looking vibrant and fresh.

Enlist Your Children

In my opinion, there's nothing as touching as a young child presenting you with a holiday gift. Regardless of the object itself, you can't help but turn to mush when a sweet young voice says "Merry Christmas" or "Happy Chanukah." So, on a Sunday two weeks before Christmas, we rolled out my daughters' fire engine–red wagon from the garage and loaded it up with the poinsettias. Then we walked from house to house making deliveries. I had one daughter ring the doorbell and the other hold the plant. They called out "Merry Christmas" in concert, as if on cue. Our good timing also meant that no one was yet frantically rushing to stores to accomplish last-minute shopping—everyone was at home to

---

Most Popular Gifts

People cluster around certain gift categories when doing their holiday shopping. According to the 2000 American Express Retail Index Survey, which polled shoppers nationwide, these are the most popular holiday gift purchases:

1. Clothing (60 percent)
2. Gift certificates and money (43 percent)
3. Entertainment items, such as books, tapes, CDs, and movies (42 percent)
4. Toys and games (37 percent)
5. Books, magazines, and magazine subscriptions (35 percent)
6. Electronics and appliances (33 percent)
7. Perfume, cologne, and cosmetics (31 percent)
8. Home furnishings and decorative items (24 percent)

---

receive our cheer. What helped make the moment even more magical was the fact that we were experiencing our first snow of the year (which I realize would be impossible for you to accomplish if you live in a warm climate).

Timing Really Is Everything

By choosing mid-December to distribute our good cheer, we were able to reach our neighbors when they were still excited about the holidays. That weekend, most people we visited were either draping their homes with lights, bringing out their ornaments, or getting ready to go out and buy a tree. They weren't worn out from holiday shopping, cooking, or planning, which made them more receptive.

Many of us have friends and relatives whom we see only during Christmas or Chanukah, so we're inevitably giving them gifts when they're already surrounded by gifts. If you want to make your effort ring out, try to plan your presentation for a unique time, as I did with the mid-December weekend.

Gift-Giving Basics

I estimate that I've purchased nearly one thousand gifts during my tenure as a gift-giving expert—and hundreds more over my lifetime. In the process, I've noted an interesting phenomenon: among all the gift-giving occasions throughout the year, buying gifts for Christmas, Chanukah, or whatever winter holiday people celebrate, causes the most anxiety. The gifts that people give at this particular time seem to have the most importance. Perhaps that's because the holidays are often the one time of the year when an entire family gets together, and everyone wants to make a good impression. Or maybe it's a societal thing, compounded by heavy-handed advertising, that almost paralyzes people about their gift-giving decisions.

⟶ The Best Gift 1 Ever Got ⟵

For me, the most meaningful gift is jewelry. When you wear that piece of jewelry, you automatically think of that person. For example, on Christmas, my daughter gave me a pair of gold earrings with a beautiful blue stone in them. They were the first piece of jewelry she'd ever given me. I love wearing them, and I always think of her whenever I do.

Judy, Maine

When I speak to groups across the country about gift giving, I hear the same question echoed: What am I going to buy my mother/sister/husband for the holidays? Over time, I've developed a sure-fire way of putting together great holiday gifts. Here are my basics.

Make a List

Jewish, Christian, Muslim, or any other religion, we can all take a tip from Santa. That is, when it comes to holiday shopping, make a list and check it twice. Or simply keep a running list of everyone to whom you intend to give something. Allow yourself a few days to accomplish this task, as names may come to you in the shower or during your commute to work, and it's best to compile all your names before you set out on the hunt. This exercise will help you in several ways:

- It gets you organized. Once you see who is on your naughty-or-nice list, you can begin to organize your efforts. You can determine what you want to buy for whom, and then plan your shopping accordingly.

- It keeps you focused. With my holiday gift list in hand this past year, I was able to streamline my shopping so that I had to visit only four stores (or the websites of those stores) to accomplish all of my gift buying. My stores of choice this year were Target, Tower Records, Amazon.com, and Harry and David.

- It helps you stay within budget. When you've got a plan of attack for your holiday acquisitions, you're much less likely to wind up in a shopping frenzy. If you've identified the CD you want to buy for your brother or the kitchen appliance that suits your aunt to a T—

> ### ⚜ The Best Gift I Ever Got ⚜
> I got a ten-speed bike for Christmas when I was sixteen. I had been beg-
> ging for one for about three years, so when I finally got it, I was thrilled. I
> eventually got rid of the bike last year when we moved—about twenty-
> seven years after I'd received it. It meant that much to me.
>
> *Therese, California*

and you've planned for the purchase financially—you're likely to
come away from your holiday shopping with your spending under
control.

Get Personal

Whenever possible, I like to choose a gift related to the recipient's
hobby—something that helps the person enjoy his or her free time more
fully. For example, as I've mentioned, I grew up in a home where refer-
encing a field guide to birds was as common as looking up a phone
number in the yellow pages. Recently, my mother retired to Maine,
where bird-watching has become an even bigger part of her day. So, I've
adjusted my gift giving for her birthday and Christmas to reflect her
expanding devotion to her hobby. Last year, we bought her a squirrel-
proof bird feeder from L.L.Bean. This year, I've already got her two new
books about birds. One is an updated field guide to replace the dog-eared
version that she's had for ages; the other is a coffee-table book on birds
from the Audubon Society (of which she's a member).

When you draw a blank on what to buy for someone — let's say, your brother-in-law — ask yourself: What does this person like to do in his free time? What are some of his hobbies? What activity do I hear him talking about? Once you have this profile, you'll know which way to head. For example, if you need to buy a gift for someone who subscribes to *The Wine Spectator* and is always on the lookout for an intriguing vintage, anything wine-related would be fitting. I've seen some stunning hand-blown glass bottle stoppers that replace a cork once the wine is opened. These stoppers do double duty as a functional item and an objet d'art. Other wine-related gifts include sturdy but beautiful goblets and nifty wine racks.

Ask Questions

One of the biggest mistakes people make when approaching gift giving is to assume that the inspiration for the perfect gift will come to them out of thin air. Nothing could be further from the truth. I always say that being a good gift giver is a lot like being a journalist: you need to be observant, and you can't be afraid to ask questions. You can sniff out the recipient's likes and dislikes with indirect queries such as "Are you doing any new hobbies these days?" or "What do you think of the new CD by (you fill in the blank)?" If the answers don't yield any gift-giving insight, then bite the bullet and ask straight out, "What would you like for the holidays?"

If you get the common (and utterly frustrating) response "Oh, I don't need anything," don't back down. Let your friends and family know that you're looking forward to buying them something and that you don't want to burden them with having to return it if it's not something they like. They may as well save themselves the trouble and suggest some gift ideas. Get them thinking by asking if there's anything they saw in a mag-

---

❧ The Best Gift I Ever Gave ❧

At my parents' house a few years ago, I came across a huge box filled with old family movies. These films dated back to the 1950s, when I was a kid. Over the next couple of weekends, my husband and I organized the more than one hundred reels in chronological order and spliced them together as a single reel. On Christmas day, we pulled out my dad's old film projector, loaded the reel, and sat back in delight as my parents watched the movie of their life together. It was a wonderful gift to give.

Leslie, New York

---

azine, on television, or in a store that appealed to them but that they couldn't justify buying. Prod them about a friend who may have some trinket or tool that they'd like to have as well. When you gently but firmly nudge them along, you'll gather the input you need.

Don't Reinvent the Wheel

I said it in the Introduction, and I reiterate it here. When you find a gift that the recipient clearly enjoys, go right ahead and give it again in following years—that is, until the recipient asks you to stop or, if it's a young person, until the gift is no longer appropriate. I strongly endorse not messing with success when it comes to gifts.

My mother gives my husband a Home Depot gift card every Christmas. She's been doing this for years, and I hope she'll continue to do so. My husband has come to expect this gift, and it makes him happier than any seemingly more "personal" gift would. That's because to my hus-

---

～❦ The Best Gift I Ever Gave ❦～

I gave my baby-sitter what I think is the best holiday gift: a night out with her husband. Inside of a handwritten card, I put two passes to the local movie theater, a gift certificate from a nearby restaurant that I know she loves, and a handmade coupon that said I would watch her kids on whatever night she wanted to go out to the movies.

Carrie, Wisconsin

---

band, a self-professed handyman, Home Depot is his shopping mecca. Receiving a gift card gives him carte blanche to go shopping for his wood shop, and that makes him utterly happy. What more could you want from a gift?

Likewise, as I disclosed in the previous chapter, I've adopted the practice of sending my business associates and corporate clients Harry and David truffles for the holidays. The yummy chocolates have proved to be a welcome antidote to the craziness that plagues businesses during December, and I hear time and again how much people enjoy receiving them—and polishing them off. Until the overwhelming response from my clients is *against* getting chocolates, I'll stay the course.

Finally, my brother-in-law struck gold with a gift for me a few years ago—a pair of earrings from a one-of-a-kind jewelry shop in New York City. They were like nothing I'd ever seen before—a dangling ruby surrounded by two tiny pearls—and I wore them almost every day that year. Before the next Christmas, my brother-in-law asked me what I wanted, and I told him, fingering my favorite earrings (which I was wearing, of course), "Another pair of earrings from that store, please." He obliged, and every Christmas since then, he's given me earrings from this fabulous shop, and every Christmas, I can't wait to open my little box of jewelry from my brother-in-law.

Shopping for Toddlers to Teens

My recommendations on buying holiday gifts for children are much the same as those outlined previously on buying birthday gifts. Here is a rundown of ways to find lots of age-appropriate gifts.

Gifts for Babies

The most important quality in a toy for a baby is safety. Refer to the Consumer Products Safety Commission website (cpsc.gov) for guidelines on

---

❧ The Best Gift I Ever Got ❧

When my family moved from the United States to Okinawa, Japan, in the 1980s, we enjoyed the fresh pineapples and other tropical fruits, but we dyed-in-the-wool New Englanders craved McIntosh apples. One Christmas, my sister, who was living in Massachusetts at the time, went out and picked two dozen McIntosh apples and had them shipped to us. Not only were these twenty-four apples rationed like water on a drifting life raft, but also we kept the shipping box in the living room for weeks afterward so the aroma of the apples would permeate the house.

Laura, Massachusetts

safe toys. Then, once you know they're safe, focus on toys that promote early-stage development—ones with handles for small fingers to grab or that make noise when shaken. Books are also an answer to the question of what to give a small child.

Gifts for Toddlers and Preschoolers

Because children this age are in high gear, toys for running, pushing, and building are a good fit. In addition to physical mobility, this is a time when a young child's imagination begins to explode, so a gift that helps the child harness her mental energy—such as dress-up clothes or a plastic tea-party set—would be prized.

Gifts for Kids in Elementary School

As kids get older and more sophisticated, so too should the toys you buy them. Now is the time to get a board game that the child can play with

---

⚘ The Best Gift I Ever Got ⚘

I've always loved the smell of real Christmas trees, but when I was growing up, my family used an artificial tree every year. One winter day, I was talking to a high school friend about how much I missed the evergreen smell of a genuine Christmas tree. Well, the next day, he came over with a small, real tree, already decorated with bows and lights. It was just the right size for me to keep in my bedroom, and I enjoyed that piney aroma every night as I drifted off to sleep.

Nicole, Mississippi

Giving Kids Gifts with Safety in Mind

According to the National Safe Kids Campaign, an organization dedicated to the prevention of childhood injury, you should keep the following safety ideas in mind when shopping for children's gifts:

- Only children over age three should receive toys with small, removable parts—they are a choking hazard. To verify that a toy is age-appropriate, check the box. Most toy manufacturers label toys that are inappropriate for kids under age three.

- Be aware of toys that could hurt children in other ways, such as those with sharp points or edges, which can cut a child, or those that make a loud noise and may damage hearing.

- Make sure that any string, strap, or cord attached to the toy is no longer than seven inches. Otherwise, it could strangle a child.

- Reserve electrical toys for kids over age eight. If the toy has a battery compartment, the compartment ideally should be kept shut with a screw, to help reduce the risk of burns.

- If you give a toy with wheels—such as a bike, a scooter, or skates—accompany it with protective gear. Nearly half a million kids visit emergency rooms each year because of accidents related to bicycles, skateboards, in-line skates, and roller skates. Such gear could include a helmet, knee pads, elbow pads, wrist guards, reflective stickers, and a horn or bell. Also, when it comes to in-line skates, one of the hardest parts of learning to use them is figuring out how to stop. Therefore, a certificate for a few introductory lessons would make a great add-on.

For more information on safe toys, visit the organization's website: safekids.org.

friends or family, such as Candy Land, Chutes and Ladders, Twister, or my daughters' new favorite, Don't Wake Daddy. If the child is familiar with computers, as more and more young children are, you can offer a fun, educational CD-ROM game or "living book."

Gifts for Teenagers

Try as one may, teens can be a challenge for conscientious gift givers. No matter how hip you think you are because you watch MTV every once in a while, unless you live and breathe the teen world, the smart money says you are totally out of touch with what's in and what's out. It's this honesty that leads me to again proclaim that the best gift for a teen is a gift certificate from a store whose depths are certain to contain something that he or she would like. Some of my favorite places to get a gift certificate for a teen include Target, Tower Records, and Amazon.com.

Intelligence Gathering

Whenever you're feeling out of the loop about what to give a child, do some basic reconnaissance. Call the parents for a briefing on what the child likes to do or any hobbies the child has. If you're comfortable asking, inquire about any specific gift suggestions or things to avoid. If you're out at a store such as Target or Toys R Us, watch kids the same age as the child for whom you're buying, and take note of the items they seem to be drawn to and what elicits the most excited reactions. If you are feeling bold, approach the accompanying fathers or mothers, explain your mission, and ask for anecdotal accounts or opinions based on their children's likes and dislikes. By surveying your target audience, you'll be sure to uncover more age-appropriate gifts than you can carry.

Gift-Giving FAQs

Q: *Inevitably, I get invited to tree-trimming parties or open houses around the holidays. I know that I'm supposed to take along some sort of gift to contribute to the festivities, but I never know what to choose. Help!*

A: It can be demanding to add party-hopping to your already overflowing "to do" list at the holidays, but to nurture your long-term relationships with friends, family, and neighbors, try to attend as many of these events as you can—even if it's for only an hour. It's a great way to spread holiday cheer, and—who knows?—you may bump into someone you haven't seen in a long time and rekindle your acquaintance. As for what to take, you have a few options that are easy to handle and not too expensive.

It never hurts to ask the host, "What can I bring?" In fact, whenever I plan a holiday party, I don't spend much time agonizing over what to serve for dessert. That's because whenever people ask what they can bring, I just reply, "A dessert." If you don't get the opportunity to inquire, I doubt anyone would turn you away if you came bearing a fruit tart or a chocolate cake.

When you're invited to a tree-trimming party, your gift solution is simple: an ornament—preferably one that reflects a hobby or personal taste of the hosts. For example, when my husband and I attended a tree trimming party given by friends who play in a band, we presented them with ornaments related to musical instruments, including a silver G-clef and a festive snare drum. If you have children, you can take them to a paint-your-own-pottery store and let them create their own ornaments for the party. And on this subject, it's thoughtful to take a special, inexpensive ornament for any children of the hosts. Too often, we overlook children when we're a guest in someone's house, and your including them in the holiday celebration will mean a lot to both the parents and the children.

When you're a guest at someone's house for a holiday party, I believe you're on solid ground with any of the following three gifts:

- *A bottle of wine.* For these purposes, I stock up on wines that are pleasing to most palates, such as chardonnay or pinot grigio (both whites). Or you can tote a bottle of Beaujolais nouveau, a French wine that is available only during the holiday season. If alcohol could be controversial, substitute sparkling cider.
- *A plant.* A Christmas cactus, a poinsettia, or any other kind of greenery is a better option than cut flowers. Why? Your hosts are probably extremely busy tending to the party, and you don't want to hand them more work —fumbling for a vase, filling it with water, and arranging the flowers. Then, they need to find a place to put it. A plant is a much lower-maintenance package.
- *A box of chocolates.* Here again, you don't want to add to your hosts' workload. A box of chocolates is perfect for passing around and sharing. And individual candies fit seamlessly into a menu. For example, your host can put them out after the meal while preparing dessert and coffee—or can choose instead to keep them for herself and enjoy them after her guests have gone home.

Q: Several members of my family have birthdays around the holidays. How can I come up with a gift for both occasions?

A: As a December birthday person myself, I think the most important thing you can do for people like me is make sure to acknowledge both the birthday and the holiday, but do it separately. One thing that drives us December birthday people crazy is getting combination presents—"Oh, here is a little something for Christmas and your birthday." It's not our fault that we were born near Christmas or Chanukah, so you shouldn't penalize the recipient by buying one gift simply because it makes your shopping easier. Use the advice offered both here and in the birthday chapter to come up with individual gifts for both occasions. Complete the picture by wrapping the birthday gift in birthday-theme paper and the holiday gift in a holiday motif so the recipient can clearly see that your intent is to honor each occasion.

Q. *In my free time, I've started making crafts and selling them at local flea markets. Is it OK to make people a gift for the holidays instead of buying something from a store?*

A: Absolutely, so long as the items you're giving are worlds beyond the Popsicle-stick crafts we all constructed at summer camp. If your wares are good enough that shoppers at a flea market want to buy them, then it sounds as if they would make lovely holiday gifts—and most people are charmed to receive something handcrafted. I always am.

My husband's stepmother can knit and sew with the best of them, and every year, she gives each of my daughters a handmade article of clothing. One year, she made them wool sweaters; another year, it was party dresses. The girls can't wait for their custom-made clothes from Granny each year. So, if you've got the professional touch, your handmade gift will make a fine impression, whether it's a framed photograph that you shot or a serving bowl that you threw in pottery class. Your friends and loved ones will cherish it for years to come, just as my daughters—and their parents—are pleased with the hand-knit sweaters and perfect dresses from Granny's design studio.

Q: *I like the idea of giving the service people in my life a small gift for the holidays, but sometimes I think they'd appreciate having the cash more. How would I figure out how much to tip them?*

A: Tipping is a tough call 365 days a year. I constantly worry that I'm tipping too well when I receive shoddy service or that I'm not tipping enough when I go out to eat or get my hair cut. I used to give out $20 bills to service people for the holidays, but I never felt comfortable doing so. Now I give tangible gifts, such as a box of chocolates, to the FedEx guy or my newspaper carrier. However, I can understand why you may want to give money instead. The people at American Express recently addressed the issue of tipping; here's what they suggest as appropriate amounts to tip people at the holidays:

- Newspaper Delivery Person—$10 to $30
- Beauty Salon Staff—$10 to $60
- Day Care Provider—$25 to $70 each, plus a small gift from your child
- Nanny—One week's pay plus a small gift from your child
- Housekeeper/Cleaning Person—$25 to $50, or one day's pay
- Regular Baby-Sitter—One evening's pay plus a small gift from your child
- Letter Carrier—They're allowed to accept gifts worth up to $20
- UPS/FedEx-like delivery person—$10 to $25
- Private Garage Attendant—$10 to $25
- Building Superintendent—$20 to $75
- Doorman—$10 to $55
- Private Trash Collector—$10 to $20 each
- Personal Trainer—One workout session's pay

~⁀ 7 ⁀~

HOUSEWARMING AND
HOSTESS GIFTS

Moving into a new home is right up there with marriage and the birth of a child as one of the pivotal events in a person's life. When my family and I moved into the home we built a little less than two years ago, it felt as if our life was finally complete. After spending the previous seven years as veritable nomads—we moved five times to four different states—it was both soothing and invigorating to settle into a place where we could finally put down roots. As friends and family began to visit, they were gracious in bringing us housewarming gifts that, in some cases, were very attractive but also practical and, in other cases, were extremely helpful as we set up house. They ranged from a rectangular ceramic serving dish from Italy to a decorative flag for the front yard to a $200 Home Depot card, which we used in earnest the first weekend after we received it.

Sending a housewarming gift is customary when you find out that someone close to you has bought a new house or moved into a new apartment. It's simple social etiquette that our moms taught us—and which I hope to reinforce here. So is the notion of a hostess gift—a little something that you give someone who invites you to dinner or to stay overnight as a guest.

Tried-and-True Gifts

If you're like me and my family, you're frequently invited for dinner at friends' homes. Because we're often being hosted, we're also often in the position of coming up with hostess gifts. To add to the comings and goings, since my husband and I are at an age when many of our friends are building or buying houses, we've been receiving a lot of "We've moved" cards of late—and sending a lot of housewarming presents. What we're not doing is running around town trying to find something "new" for each of these occasions. As I've asserted all along, I don't believe in reinventing the wheel every time I'm obliged to give a gift. Instead, we've identified a handful of tried-and-true housewarming and hostess gifts to which we can turn whenever we need them. Here are a few of the best ones.

Wine

A nice bottle of wine works well as both a housewarming and a hostess gift, and it's my gift of choice when I go to someone's house for dinner. An easy and effective way to approach choosing a wine is to keep your eyes and ears open for recommendations.

For example, when you dine out and are served a particularly satisfying bottle of white or red, write down all the information from the label before the waiter takes the bottle away. Don't rely on your memory or a mental image of the logo, since subtle details can make major differences in taste as well as price. Or, do as I did recently: after indulging in a particularly fine glass of wine at a restaurant, I asked our waiter for more information on the vintage. Not only did she write down the name and year, but she included the price and where I could buy it locally. Another handy and reliable source is the "Weekend Journal" section of the *Wall Street Journal*, which has a widely read wine column. It's not at all highbrow and is so well written that even an amateur can get valuable tidbits on worthy bottles of wine, as I have many times.

When you identify a wine, check out your local liquor store. It may take a few tries, but once you find what you're looking for, stock up on it. (Think gift closet, but the wine cellar variety.) Then, the next time you're invited to someone's house for dinner, you won't have to scramble for a hostess gift. You can just grab one of those highly recommended bottles from your stash.

When it comes to a housewarming gift, I'd still suggest giving wine but with a twist: give a personal vintage. No, I'm not suggesting that you invest in oversize vats and start pressing your own Chianti. Rather, send

---

⚜ The Best Gift I Ever Got ⚜

When my husband and I moved into our house, a business associate gave us a generous gift certificate from a local nursery as a housewarming gift. We bought a bunch of small fruit trees. That was five years ago. Today we have a thriving orchard of citrus, plums, and nectarines. Mmmm!

Miriam, California

a message on a bottle by ordering from a winery that will custom-design the label, and print your good wishes alongside the vintage. For example, your label might read, "From our house to yours. Congratulations. Love, John and Sue." Here are three wineries with mail-order operations that excel at this kind of personalized gift. (Note: These companies ship to only certain areas of the country where interstate transport of alcohol is allowed, so check first before settling on mail-order wine as your housewarming gift of choice.)

Chaddsford Winery

This boutique winery, headquartered in the picturesque Brandywine Valley, southeast of Philadelphia, offers custom labeling on four of its wines: Proprietors Reserve White, Chardonnay, Proprietors Red, and Sunset Blush. You can order full- or half-bottle sizes, with a one-case minimum. In addition to the price of the wines, Chaddsford charges $85 for up to 150 labels. If you live in the Philadelphia region and want to taste any of the wines before ordering, you'll find tasting rooms in Peddler's Village in Bucks County and Manayunk in the city of brotherly love. The main number for Chaddsford headquarters, where you place custom-label orders, is (610) 388-6221.

New Hope Winery

At this Bucks County, Pennsylvania, winery, you can choose a custom label for any of its twenty-five varieties. They include reds, whites, and blushes, as well as seasonal and specialty wines, which run the gamut from red sangria to Dutch apple spice (a spiked apple cider). All orders have a one-case minimum. You can pay for a case of wine and customize all the labels to be the same for a $3.50-per-bottle charge, or, for

---

Gift Giving FYI

A wonderful housewarming gift for someone who has bought a new house is a custom-crafted address sign that can be hung on the garage or displayed on the front lawn. While you can order these from most home improvement stores, I admire the variety of signs available from the Improvements catalog, all of which are made of rust-free aluminum but decorated to look like either brass or ceramic. Each sign features raised letters for easy reading and which won't fade over time, as stick-on letters do. You can select from many shapes, including a brass-like rectangular sign and an oblong ceramic-style one. Prices start at about $43. Call (800) 642-2112, or visit the company's website at improvementscatalog.com.

---

a nominal fee, you can vary the labels. While you can select the wine and a label design through the company's website at newhopewinery.com, a representative will finalize your order the old-fashioned way—by calling you to take credit card and shipping information. Or you can do the whole thing over the phone at (800) 592-WINE (9463).

Windsor Vineyards

Windsor holds the distinction of being the first winery to offer custom-created labels, and what makes Windsor vintages noteworthy is that they are grown and bottled in Sonoma County, in California's renowned wine country. What's also important is that your custom order can be as small as two bottles. You have forty varieties from which to choose, including classics such as cabernet and chardonnay as well as dessert wines and champagne. Call (800) 333-9987, or visit Windsor Vineyards on-line at windsorvineyards.com.

Housewares

We have dear friends whom we have known since high school. These friends have brought or sent us a housewarming gift each time we moved—whether it was from one New York City apartment to another or across the country. Each time, they gave us housewares of some sort. One move, it was pretty ceramic candlestick holders. Another time, it was a glass vase. For each of the last two moves (I told you we've moved a lot), they gave us a green-and-white-speckled serving bowl, part of a matched set. The first bowl, to commemorate our move to a new home in New Jersey, is oversize and round, with scalloped edges. The second bowl is shallow and square—a variation on the traditional pasta bowl. We love these serving dishes, and we keep them on display in our kitchen. When we've entertained, they've held everything from potato chips to salad to pasta. This year, we even used the square bowl for our Halloween candy.

You can see why a serving bowl of some sort makes an unbeatable housewarming gift: it performs multiple functions—from adorning a

---

⇜ The Best Gift I Ever Gave ⇝

Because my line of work requires that I travel to Paris a lot, I like to stock up on a certain brand of hand cream that's available only in France. I usually buy it in bulk and then give it as a hostess gift when I'm invited to someone's house. It's a refreshing alternative to the usual wine or flowers, and the fact that it comes from Paris makes it "ooh-la-la."

Donna, New Jersey

Gift Giving FYI

Want a practical housewarming gift for the family that has everything? How about pre-paying their bills? The *Wall Street Journal* recently reported that a short list of utility companies across the country allow friends and family members to buy gift certificates to cover someone's utility bills—for a month or an entire year. One Iowa family spent $480 on such gift certificates for their newly married son and daughter-in-law. So far, utility companies in Florida, Tennessee, Connecticut, and Iowa offer this program.

---

shelf to holding sweets for trick-or-treaters. This versatility makes it one of my go-to housewarming gifts. I'm partial to bowls made of ceramic, painted in bright colors, and large enough to be used for a mound of salad or spaghetti. In fact, I just picked up one to send to those friends from high school, who moved into a new home of their own.

When you're on your housewares-buying quest, here's a question to consider: Do your friends collect a certain kind of dishes or material? If so, try to find a piece that goes with the collection. For example, we're big Fiestaware fans. We're drawn to the bright colors of our set and the fact that the design is versatile and will match most anything—including the beloved green-and-white serving bowls I told you about. We use Fiestaware for our everyday dishes and have been collecting serving pieces for the set over the years. Several family members who know of our fondness for Fiestaware chose it as a housewarming gift for us. It was exactly what we wanted and needed, and their obvious effort to reflect our tastes imparted a personal sincerity—which you want for your housewarming gift whenever possible.

Try to plan your purchases to take advantage of opportunities to build your on-hand supplies. If you travel to a place where unique housewares can be found at a good price, leave some room in your suit-case, and load up while you're there. A few years ago, I had to travel to eastern Europe for business, and I discovered before I left that glass from Poland and Hungary was well regarded in the United States. I knew I'd stumbled onto a promising source for a supply of housewarm-ing gifts, so while I was in Warsaw, Krakow, and Budapest, I focused in on inexpensive suppliers of quality glass housewares. I ended up at one shop in Warsaw that had a dazzling assortment of brightly colored hand-blown glass vases for about three American dollars, and I bought enough to fill a large shopping bag. Later in Budapest, I came across a shop with floor-to-ceiling shelves of wine goblets reminiscent of Tiffany glass. I think I stuffed a giant suitcase with those glasses, and for about a year, I had a ready supply of first-rate housewarming gifts with the added flair of having been purchased overseas.

Gift-Giving FAQ

Q: What do you give to the hosts when you stay at their house?

A: First, let me compliment you on wanting to thank the hosts for hosting you in their home by giving them a gift. This and the thank-you note are two rules of eti-quette that have slipped away from modern day life. Now, what to buy.

Fortunately, when you've been a guest in someone's home, you've had the leisure to observe how the hosts live and what objects they keep around. This inside look should be a good place to start when you decide what type of gift to send by way of thanks.

For instance, my husband and I recently stayed with friends who I had thought of as your average coffee drinkers, but upon spending a few days with them, I dis-covered that they were true java aficionados. So, the thank-you-for-hosting-us gift we sent was all about coffee: a quartet of oversize mugs made from funky-painted pottery, packaged with a bag of premium beans. I know the gift hit the spot because they called as soon as it arrived to thank *us* for sending it.

Another time, I stayed with a work colleague in Chicago while we attended a sales meeting in the city. I learned while I was with her that she was allergic to wheat and had a heck of a time finding ingredients for cakes and cookies that she could bake and enjoy. When I returned to New York, I made the rounds of a few health food stores and purchased a selection of wheat-free muffin, cake, and cookie mixes, which I then tucked into an attractive basket and sent off to my colleague. The thank-you note I received from her was one of the most endearing anyone has ever written to me.

Think back on your visit at someone's home to any comments or conversations during your stay that speak to your host's likes or dislikes. Or if your visit has yet to happen, try to keep your gift-giving radar on alert throughout your visit. Did your friend show interest in a book you were reading and remark that she'd been meaning to read it? Buy her a copy when you get home. Was your host planning a vacation? Purchase something fun and appropriate for the trip—maybe sunblock and a straw hat for someone heading to the tropics, or a guidebook with a colorful bookmark that pertains to the city or region.

If all your investigating does not lead you to the right gift, you can go with the vast array of housewares, notepaper, or candles that I recommend you keep stocked in your gift closet and use one of these as your hostess gift.

~ 8 ~

GIFT GIVING FOR LOVERS, MOMS, DADS, AND GRADS

This chapter takes you through some annual gift-giving occasions that aren't full-blown shopping holidays but nonetheless warrant a suggestion. They are Valentine's Day, Mother's Day, and Father's Day. In addition, every spring thousands of students graduate from high school and college, and chances are you'll be invited to a graduation party sometime in the near future. You won't have to pull an all-nighter in search of a grade-A gift after reviewing this chapter.

You Gotta Have Heart: Valentine's Day

If you're lucky enough to have been pierced by cupid's arrow, then you know how your heart races to find the right gift for Valentine's Day. I can still remember being a single twenty-something when I found myself with a boyfriend for the first time ever on Valentine's Day. (High school boyfriends never counted as much, since I didn't have a disposable income to use when shopping for a gift.) Since I'd never been in a long-

---

❧ The Best Gift I Ever Got ❧

When I was newly married, I had to go on a business trip, and I happened to be away on Valentine's Day. When I arrived at my destination, an employee at the site I was visiting handed me an envelope with my name on it. Inside was a Valentine's Day card from my husband, who had gone through the trouble of sending this card ahead of time so that it would be waiting for me when I arrived.

Anne, North Carolina

---

term relationship, I was clueless about what to give him. We weren't very serious at the time, so I didn't want to come off as too romantic. But I didn't want to let the day go by without any recognition whatsoever. So, what did I wind up getting him? A simple wood frame that was painted red and contained a picture of me. I figured he could put it on his desk at work or somewhere in his apartment. He seemed pleased with the gift I gave him, and I loved the cotton T-shirt with tiny red hearts all over it that he got for me. In fact, I wore it for years after we'd broken up and eventually relegated it to workout clothes when it became worn-out. A few years and holes later, I finally let it go.

Put Some Zing in the Heartstring

For so many couples, Valentine's Day equals chocolates in a heart-shape box and a bouquet of red roses. Both are time-honored gifts—and ones I've been happy to receive since the first Valentine's Day with my husband. If you have your heart set on a classically romantic gift for him or her, chocolates and roses are all that. So is a candlelit dinner at a favorite restaurant, and one I would recommend for a food lover. But if you're aiming to give a Valentine's Day gift with a twist, here are some that should be a hit.

C Is for Cookie

A standout gift for your sweetie is a cookie bouquet, which is just what it sounds like: cookies arranged to resemble a bouquet of flowers. You can visit a local bakery and put the arrangement together yourself, or call in the experts. One company I frequently use is Cookies by Design, which offers a basket of oversize cookies shaped and decorated to look like red roses, or one with heart-shape cookies covered with red icing—both perfect for Valentine's Day. You can choose your design and locate a Cookies by Design franchise nearest you by visiting the company's website at cookiebouquet.com. Currently, there are 213 such shops in 43 states. Seven-cookie arrangements start at $35.

Raise a Glass

Toast your love by raising a glass of champagne to each other. But don't just pop the bubbly and drink up. Instead, put together a gift of love that

---

Valentine's Day Quick Tip

Plan to shop after-Valentine's Day sales to stock up on heart-related and red-hued items at closeout prices. These can come in handy in a number ways. Children can use juvenile-looking materials for Valentine's Day gifts for their friends next year. You can put aside heart-shape picture frames for bridal shower gifts. And you can adapt anything red that you've purchased for your holiday decorating, stocking stuffing, and gift giving come next December.

⁓ *The Best Gift 1 Ever Got* ⤳

On the first Valentine's Day after my boyfriend (now husband) and I started dating, he conspired with my then-roommate to let him into our house while I was at work. He filled my bedroom with red and white helium balloons, replaced the white lightbulbs in my lamps with red ones, and left a dozen roses on my bed. On this particularly bad day, I came home from work and opened my bedroom door to find more than six dozen balloons floating inside. It was fantastic. The best part was what I found out later: he'd had to make six trips back and forth to the florist to transport all of the balloons in his tiny car.

Gwen, New Jersey

---

contains a pair of crystal champagne flutes, a small box of chocolate-dipped strawberries or chocolate candy, and a personalized bottle of champagne. You can order the latter (technically, sparkling wine, since only the French can call this bubbly spirit champagne) from Windsor Vineyards, a Sonoma County winery that has been offering personalized labels on all of its wines since it began its mail-order operations in 1959 (see Chapter 7). There is no extra charge for the three-line personalized label. To contact Windsor Vineyards call (800) 333-9987 or go on-line at windsorvineyards.com.

Anything (Heart-Shape) Goes

Around Valentine's Day, stores overflow with all things heart-shape or featuring hearts—crystal bowls, boxes of candy, picture frames, clothing—

and any one of these work well as a Valentine's Day gift. You can outfit a guy in boxer shorts with hearts on them or a gal in heart-print pajamas. If your sweetheart is more of a jewelry person, go with a pair of heart-shape earrings or a necklace with a heart-shape charm. If your guy wears shirts with French cuffs, give him heart-shape cuff links or, if that's too over the top for him, cuff links with a ruby red center. For the pint-size set, a teacher gift that's both inexpensive and thoughtful is a heart-shape red candle. By going with the heart theme, you're sure to find a great Valentine's Day gift.

Plan a Romantic Getaway

A wonderful way to enjoy Valentine's Day together is to escape to a romantic getaway. Arrange to have someone watch your kids, if necessary, and go away for the weekend like newlyweds.

I know of one man who took his wife away on Valentine's Day but didn't tell her where they were going. He told her to pack warm-weather clothing—her first hint, since they live in a cold climate—but that was the only clue he'd offer. It wasn't until they'd arrived at Miami International Airport that she discovered they were taking a weekend cruise.

If your finances won't allow something as extravagant as a cruise, economize in romantic style by spending the weekend at a bed and breakfast or country inn. If you live in a city, you can book a weekend at a downtown hotel and play tourist for a change. Order room service, sleep late, and go sight-seeing.

Have a Heart-Healthy Holiday

While a heart-shape cutout is the ultimate Valentine's Day symbol, a healthful way to present a Valentine's Day gift is with the old ticker itself in mind. Here are some heart healthy ways to celebrate:

Give and eat chocolate. Chocolate lovers worldwide rejoiced recently when medical studies showed that chocolate contains antioxidants, the cancer-fighting substance also found in fruits and vegetables. In fact, the U.S. Department of Agriculture and the *Journal of the American Chemical Society* reported that two of the foods with the highest concentration of antioxidants are dark chocolate and milk chocolate. In addition, chocolate does not contain cholesterol, and the monosaturated oleic acid found in chocolate has been shown to reduce cholesterol.

Get moving. An invigorating way to celebrate Valentine's Day is to get physical with the one you love. Spend the afternoon hiking in the woods, or make a date at the local ice-skating rink, where you can glide hand-in-hand like high school sweethearts. Or you could participate in a race that benefits a good cause—ideally, alongside the people you love. Each year, several races are held on or near Valentine's Day, with the proceeds helping to fund a local charity. For example, one year, the Annual Valentine Road Race in Bradford, New Hampshire, helped to raise funds to restore a church in town. Husbands and wives along with mothers and daughters ran together. You can locate a Valentine's Day race near you by checking out the *Runner's World* magazine website at runnersworld.com, which lists races nationwide.

Putting Parents First: Mother's Day and Father's Day

It's probably the same old story every year: when you think about what to give the folks for Mother's and Father's Day, you quickly arrive at flowers for her and a tie for him. Perhaps, that's because you know that your mom can't get enough flowers and your dad is always short on nifty new ties to go with his suits. Without a doubt, continue sending those splendid floral arrangements each Mother's Day and those eye-catching ties on Father's Day if that's what they like.

As I've said before, if you give a gift that is well received, don't stop. There's no reason to start from scratch with each gift-giving occasion just because you're reluctant to repeat yourself. After all, most people don't prize variety for its own sake; they want to get gifts that they'll use and enjoy. If you know that your mother or father (or a grandparent, for that matter) used and enjoyed your previous years' gifts, then don't mess with success. While you may tell yourself that you should give your parents something different, if it's pretty to look at but not practical, it may sit in a box at the bottom of the closet—only to be brought out and displayed hours before you come over for a visit. That's not how you want people to feel about a gift you've given—that it's an obligation to accommodate. You want them to genuinely enjoy it.

If you discover that your previously loved gifts are no longer so successful, that's a different story line. Mom has developed allergies to flowers, or Dad's office has gone business casual. The easiest thing to do is apply the gift-giving strategies from previous chapters. Here's a brief recap.

Check with Your Sources

If you've learned that flowers and ties are out, ask Mom and Dad what they'd really like as a gift. If they balk and say, "Oh, I have everything I need," assure them that you're going to give them a gift regardless and that, since you want to get something for Mother's Day or Father's Day that they'll use and enjoy, they should volunteer some ideas. If that doesn't pan out, then start asking questions.

Again, like a reporter, you need to be observant and unafraid to ask questions. So give these a whirl:, "Are there any books you've been meaning to read that I can buy for you?" or "Did you enjoy a nice bottle of wine recently that you'd like to have in the house?" or "Is there any restaurant nearby where you've wanted to eat? Maybe I can make reservations for us."

Tie in a Hobby

The hobbies or pastimes your mom or dad enjoys can be a springboard to excellent gifts. My mother the bird-watcher is also an avid gardener. So, if I wanted to give her flowers for Mother's Day, I probably wouldn't send a bouquet from the florist (although I'm sure she'd find them pretty). Rather, more appropriate for her would be a flat of annuals that she could plant in her garden. And if I could arrange it, I'd spend Mother's Day with her, digging in the dirt.

Does your dad have a fondness for going to the movies? If so, offer to take him to the latest release on Father's Day and then out to eat at his favorite restaurant. If you don't live nearby, send him a gift certificate to the movies, or a gift card from a local video store so he can enjoy seeing a film as a gift from you.

Offer an Indulgence

If there's one universal truth about parents, it's that they don't often indulge themselves as much as they should. To remedy this situation, circle Mother's Day and Father's Day on your calendar as the perfect time to give them a gift of indulgence. Choose a box of chocolates for either parent or, if you think they'd appreciate and use it, a certificate for an afternoon of pampering at a nearby spa. For a parent who lives alone or has a busy schedule, arrange for a cleaning service to take care of the house or for a catering service to deliver meals so Mom or Dad doesn't have to cook for a few days. All of these gifts say "Take a well-earned break" and should soothe the body as well as the spirit.

If You've Got Children, Use Them for Inspiration

My husband and I can both attest that as far as our own moms and dads are concerned, anything made by or featuring their grandchildren is a gift worth more than gold. If you've got children and your mind is blocked about what would be a good Mother's Day or Father's Day gift, look to the kids for inspiration. We have a paint-your-own pottery store nearby where kids can create a vase, candy dish, or jewelry box. If I were ever at a loss for a Mother's Day or Father's Day gift, I'd bring my children to this store and set them loose making something for their grandmother or grandfather.

Pictures of your children, always a solid gift for parents, take the cake on Mother's Day or Father's Day. Snap some photos of your children in front of a pretty spring-like background and then place those shots in a frame. If you want to commemorate the occasion, buy a frame that says "Happy Mother's Day 2002" or something like that.

Give What You Enjoy

When in doubt, a good resort is to give something you enjoy. If you've read a book that you think Mom or Dad would find compelling, buy another copy as your gift. Do the same with a CD or a bottle of wine. Enclose a handwritten note that explains why you've chosen the gift— that you recently enjoyed the same thing, and you thought your mom or dad would have a similarly positive reaction.

Welcome to the Real World: Graduation

When I graduated from college, my parents got together and bought me a computer. It was the perfect present for me since I had just earned a degree in journalism, and I knew I wanted to pursue freelance writing. The best way for me to do that was to have the latest computer technology at home. I used and abused that computer, and eventually I upgraded to an even better model. I couldn't have launched my professional writing career without that old, now obsolete computer, which is why it's one of my never-to-be-forgotten gifts.

Get Technical

One of the best gifts you can give a graduating high school or college senior is a computer. Many colleges require incoming freshmen to have certain technology at their disposal, so a computer gift helps send a college-bound teen off fully equipped. Likewise, most college graduates heading out into the real world rely on a home computer to surf the Net for jobs or just for E-mailing.

If swinging the entire purchase is too much for you, going in with a couple of friends or family members can make it an affordable group gift. Of course, don't go computer shopping without first checking with the graduate's parents. They may be planning to buy a computer themselves for their son or daughter, rendering your gift redundant. In that event, one of these related options could be the perfect solution:

- Find out the machine's specs and give compatible software, such as an accounting program for keeping track of finances.

- Offer to buy a printer or scanner.

- Buy a half dozen or so printer cartridges and a ream of paper, both pricey parts that will surely come in handy down the road.

- Give a gift certificate to a store where the graduate can get electronics supplies and accessories.

- Give a gift certificate to an E-tailer, so the graduate can inaugurate the computer by doing some on-line shopping.

Sweep Them Away with Housewares

Both high school and college graduates often find themselves in new quarters—a dormitory or apartment—where their houseware needs instantly increase. For these transplants, a gift of housewares can save them time and money.

A lifesaving gift I received before going off to college—and which I've subsequently given to high school graduates many times over—was a laundry basket filled with dormitory necessities: hangers, toothbrush holder, iron, desktop mirror, a gallon of laundry detergent, and an alarm clock. You can fill up your own basket or tub based on the needs of the recipient. Then, to wrap it up, buy a large roll of cellophane and create the perfect gift basket secured with ribbon or a bow.

For the college graduate, anything that can help furnish a first apartment or home would be welcomed. A set of contemporary cooking pots or baking pans are essentials, as are bed linens or bath towels. If you're unsure what the person wants or likes, go with a gift certificate to a home furnishings store.

Dress Them for Success

While I was more than grateful for the computer that my parents gave me for my college graduation, what I could have used as well was some help updating my wardrobe—or at least some guidance on how to dress for job interviews. I still cringe when I think back at what a fashion emergency I was. I had no idea what kind of jacket to wear, or that investing in new clothes would not only make me look professional but increase my confidence as well. Thus, I think a smart gift for college

---

❧ The Best Gift I Ever Gave ❧

I had a really close-knit group of friends in college. Right before graduation, I put together a photo album of pictures of us—from freshman to senior years. I added quotes and inside jokes underneath each picture. Then I made five color copies of the book so I could give one to each of my friends. I put a different cover on each album, and then wrote a personal letter to my friend on the last page. That was my graduation gift to all, and even now, years later when we get together, we'll all reminisce using this handmade photo album.

Staci, New York

> ~~≈ **The Best Gift 1 Ever Gave** ≈~~
>
> The gift that I love to give to graduates is a world globe. I love to travel, and I love to encourage others to do so as well. A globe introduces the concept of the world and is a great way to whet the person's appetite to travel to various places.
>
> *Katharine, Quebec*

graduation is a gift certificate from a store with a line of business clothes. Department stores qualify, as do high-end retailers such as Ann Taylor and Banana Republic. The college graduate in question may also benefit from the services of a personal shopper, which could be a considerate add-on to your gift certificate.

Make It Money

If you can't determine a specific gift, go with greenbacks. A student who'll be entering college can use it to buy books, and the college grad can apply it to car payments, rent, or travel expenses.

Instead of just slipping a check in an envelope, be a little creative with how you package the gift. For example, with a college-bound graduate, find out which school the student will be attending, and then buy a mug or baseball cap with that school's name or insignia, and place the cash gift inside. For a college graduate who will be traveling to a new location to start a job, package your gift with fun items that represents the move—a foldout map of the new city, a used airline ticket envelope, or a video that's representative of the new town or line of work, such as

"All the President's Men" for the fresh-faced new journalist or "When Harry Met Sally" for someone moving to the Big Apple.

Gift Giving FYI

The Lenox Gift Company, which is best known for its china and porcelain collectibles, recently amassed a history of gift giving. Here's what the company found out about the tradition of Mother's Day and Father's Day:

☞ The first Mother's Day was observed on May 10, 1908, in Grafton, West Virginia. People gathered at church there to honor a local schoolteacher's deceased mother and, by extension, all the mothers who attended the service. That teacher, Anna Jarvis, eventually lobbied the federal government to declare Mother's Day a national holiday. She got her wish six years later when President Woodrow Wilson signed a proclamation that the second Sunday in May was to be Mother's Day.

☞ In honor of Mother's Day each year, Americans purchase 10 million bouquets of flowers and exchange 150 million greeting cards. It seems that taking Mom out for a meal is a popular gift, since more people eat out at restaurants on Mother's Day than on any other day of the year.

☞ Father's Day also had its simple start at a church service in West Virginia. In 1910, a woman named Sonora Smart Dodd realized that her father had sacrificed much to raise her and her five siblings after her mother had died, and that he, like other fathers, deserved a day of tribute. Dodd began a letter-writing campaign to promote the idea of Father's Day, which she proposed be on her father's birthday, June 5.

☞ Once Mother's Day was accepted as a holiday, the push was on for Father's Day to be recognized equally. Both Presidents Woodrow Wilson and Calvin Coolidge tried to convince Congress of the need for Father's Day, but it wasn't until 1972 that President

Richard Nixon officially declared that the second Sunday in June be nationally recognized as Father's Day.

🐚 Father's Day founder Dodd suggested that the rose be the flower of Father's Day—a white rose to honor a deceased father, and a red rose to honor a living father. While we don't hear much about roses and fathers, the rose is considered the flower of choice for Father's Day.

🐚 Americans buy about 95 million Father's Day cards each year, but only about 16 percent of them take Dad out for a meal that day.

❧ 9 ❧

WHAT TO DO FOR
WEDDINGS

Weddings are perhaps the least complex present-buying situation: the couple registers for gifts, and you use that registry as a printed guide. Or, if you live in an area where giving money is more accepted than giving china, you write out a check, and you're all set. But chances are, the wedding isn't the only time you'll be giving the happy couple a gift. Before anyone walks down the aisle, you'll probably get invitations to engagement parties and at least one bridal shower. Between the betrothal and the ceremony itself, you're going to be doing a lot of shopping.

While I advocate giving repeat gifts—or at least ones that are related—when they've gone over big for birthdays and holidays, I make an exception for the series of gifts for an engagement party, a bridal shower, and then a wedding. Sure, it might be efficient to purchase three place settings of the couple's china and then give one for each occasion. However, when the bride and groom review their gift list as they write their thank-you notes—and trust me, they will be keeping a list—they will probably find it rather odd that you gave the same thing three times. Assuming "oddball" is not quite the impression you'd hoped to make, this chapter offers some old, new, borrowed, and blue ideas for each of the gift-giving scenarios you're likely to encounter when a friend, colleague, or relative ties the knot.

Engagement Gifts

When my husband and I got engaged, I was pleased when people sent me congratulations cards, but I was really touched when we received unexpected engagement gifts. Now, understand that you're not expected to send an engagement gift when someone announces the big news, although it's nice if you can. However, if you are invited to an engagement party (which oftentimes turns into a mini-wedding), it's absolutely

---

⇜ The Best Gift I Ever Gave ⇝

For my sister, I put together a bridal gift that was a box of household hints, which I'd collected over the years. Each hint was taped to the substance that you would use to solve a household dilemma. For example, to a bottle of vinegar I taped "Pour vinegar over your hands to eliminate onion odors." Years later, she told me that whenever she or her husband was faced with a household quandary, her husband would tell her to look at my box to see if there was an answer there.

Marty, New York

expected that you take a gift. If you can't attend the festivities, you should at least send a little something to commemorate the newly announced engagement.

Wedding-Planning Books

One of my favorite engagement gifts was a wedding-planning book from my maid of honor. She gave it to me almost immediately after our announcement, and before I'd had the chance to go to the bookstore myself and start perusing the wedding racks. While I still wound up buying additional guides to match my specific needs, this general how-to on wedding basics was an indispensable tool, and a gift to consider for any newly engaged woman.

Once of the reasons I loved that wedding-planning book is that it laid out everything I needed to know to organize myself and to do a better job of lining up the vendors I would have to hire—a caterer, a photographer, and more. I recently came across that trusty planner, and I found myself reading all the notes I'd written to myself in the margins about things I wanted at my wedding. It also contained pictures of hats and shoes that I admired and hoped to buy, which I'd clipped from magazines and slipped between the pages. Revisiting that book was like taking the proverbial stroll down memory lane; it jogged memories of my wedding in a way photographs never could, because it allowed me to go inside my head and relive what I was thinking and going through at the time. It also reminded me how much the gift meant to me—and still does.

If you're going to buy a book that's primarily for the bride's use, complement the gift by buying a book for the groom as well. Among the possibilities is a hilarious book written by my very funny friend Dan Zevin called *The Nearly Wed Handbook*. Imagine if the cable-TV net-

work Comedy Central produced a wedding-planning program, and
you'll get a pretty good idea of Dan's book—it's tailor-made reading for
the guy.

Picture Frames

Another noteworthy engagement gift we received was a pretty pewter
frame. First Bill and I put our engagement picture in the frame; then
we put our wedding portrait in it. That framed portrait is still promi-

---

Gift Giving FYI

While I'm a huge advocate of shopping off the bride and groom's registry list, there
are times when shopping from the actual *store* where the couple registered is out of
the question. If you don't live near the merchant at which the couple is registered—
and that merchant doesn't offer an on-line or catalog shopping option—then a good
place to find an item is the Ross-Simons catalog. This Rhode Island–based cataloger
has come through in a pinch for me many times when I wanted a place setting of china
for someone but, for whatever reason, the specified store wasn't going to work for me.
Ross-Simons was even a lifesaver for guests at my own wedding, when the Lenox china
I'd requested was back-ordered at other stores. Ross-Simons had it in stock, available
for immediate shipping, *and* at a price that was about 20 percent less than what the
department stores were charging.

The company is also a reliable source for silver, crystal, jewelry, linens, and other
decorative housewares that make terrific housewarming gifts. As a bonus, the catalog has its own gift registry program, which is a wonderful choice when you're getting
married and want to give your guests across the country no-hassle access to *your* registry. To receive a Ross-Simons catalog call (800) 458-4545 or visit the on-line store at
ross-simons.com.

---

nently displayed in our home. The combination of functionality, versatility, and sentimental attachment makes a picture frame a timeless engagement gift.

Buying off the Registry

If the newly engaged couple is really on the ball, they might already have registered for gifts, which means you have another option for choosing an engagement gift. If this is the case, one of the smaller, more personal items on the registry would be fine. Here again, perhaps a picture frame.

If the couple has registered for some funky stuff, like margarita glasses or other fun barware, you can buy four or eight of the glasses, and then package them with a recipe guide on making the perfect margarita or martini, along with an accompanying bottle of liquor. Or, give them the glasses, a blender, and a "Smoothies Deck," which is a set of recipes packaged like a deck of cards that show you how to make fifty different delicious drinks (some alcoholic). You can order the "Smoothies Deck" from the Femail Creations catalog for $13 by calling (800) 996-9223, or visit the website at femailcreations.com.

Gifts That Give Stress Relief

As soon as a couple starts putting together a wedding "to do" list, the old blood pressure starts going up. This is the best time for a gift that lets them blow off steam, or at least relax. You'll do both if you treat them to a couple's massage, which many spas today offer, so they can savor some downtime together. Or collaborate with a group of friends and pay for a restful weekend away at a country inn. For some serious blowing-off-steam, you could purchase certificates for a set of kickboxing or karate classes to take together, or give them the gift of laughter, which is a great stress reliever, by treating them to a night out at a comedy club.

Bridal Showers

I'm always pleased when a bridal shower has a theme, because it makes getting a gift for the occasion so much easier. If, say, you're invited to a kitchen-themed event, you know to direct your thoughts to cookware or other culinary items. (Ideally, the couple will have registered, and you can scan the official wish list for everything in the kitchen.) If you go to a lingerie bridal shower, the gift field is equally obvious: something sexy, something slinky, something for the bedroom. But what is the right gift for when you've been invited to a regular old bridal shower—one for which there's no theme, and is perhaps in honor of a bride you don't know well, like your new husband's second cousin's fiancée? Here are some tried-and-true tips for buying great bridal shower gifts.

Consult the Registry

Most shower invitations these days come with information about where the couple has registered. If yours doesn't, find out where the bride is registered by calling the shower hostess or asking the parents, if you know them. Then, your only quandary is how much to spend.

A single place setting of china is usually in most people's price range—that is, if the bride and groom were thoughtful when registering. It drives me crazy when I get a copy of a registry and realize that the bride and groom obviously had no qualms about asking for everything expensive in the store—and no consideration of the fact that different people have different budgets for wedding gifts. That's why I always advise couples to register for a wide price range of items. By doing so, you give people the option of going all out and buying you the $500 soup tureen or simply getting you a $25 picture frame.

If you're staring at a registry list with only high-priced items on it, you have two choices: one, find other people to go in on the gift with you, which will allow you to buy more and have everyone spend less; or two, buy a nonregistry gift—one with a price tag that doesn't send your budget into a nosedive.

⁓⊱ The Best Gift I Ever Gave ⊰⁓

When my best friend and his wife got engaged, they registered for gifts at a cookware store. Ordinarily, I shop off the registry, since I figure people know best what they want and need. However, this was a special friend, and I wanted to make a special effort—particularly since I knew they both had crazy schedules and often ate frozen dinners cooked in the microwave. I decided to give them a gift that would help them appreciate any high-end kitchen gadgets they'd be receiving from their registry: a personal chef, albeit for the short term. Through a local cooking school, I arranged to have a chef come to their home and use their cookware to prepare food and to demonstrate his techniques every step of the way. The idea was to leave them with several fast-but-healthy recipes and some new culinary skills. Needless to say, this gift was a huge hit, and they still remark that it was one of the best gifts they received.

Fawn, California

Gift-Giving FAQs

Q: I have to give a wedding gift to two somewhat "offbeat" people, and I don't think they want a regular wedding gift. I want to give them something, but I don't know where to start. Help!

A: The first thing you need is to find out if the couple registered. While you say that this duo is "offbeat," even the most artsy of couples have been known to register their gift preferences, usually to comply with family wishes. So, ask, and you may just receive a solution to your gift-giving dilemma.

What if they *didn't* register? Well, then, you've got some investigating to do. Start asking yourself some questions about this couple, assuming that you know them well. (If you don't, I've got a standard gift to give, but more about that later.) How is their home decorated? What do they like to do in their free time? What are their careers? Answers to these questions can guide you in your gift search. For example, if this couple is very down-to-earth and enjoys outdoorsy activities, a gift certificate to any store that promotes an active lifestyle is probably a safe bet. Retailers such as L.L.Bean, REI, and Eastern Mountain Sports spring to mind. If they like to cook or entertain, you may want to pick something kitchen-related from Williams-Sonoma, Crate & Barrel, or Pottery Barn. (Note: I'm mentioning national stores because of their countrywide access, but that doesn't mean that you can't shop locally. I'm a proponent of supporting local, small businesses, so if you frequent one that may fulfill your gift-giving needs, by all means shop there.)

As for the standard gift I promised you, buy something from Tiffany. Your gift will come packaged in Tiffany's trademark robin's egg blue box and tied with a crisp white ribbon, and it's bound to be a big hit with the recipients. My favorite I-don't-know-you-very-well-but-I-wanted-you-to-have-a-nice-engagement/wedding-gift purchase is Tiffany's crystal ice bucket (about $80, last time I looked).

*Q: I know it's important to buy a wedding gift off the couple's registry, but I'm a procras-
tinator. As a consequence, by the time I get around to finding a copy of the list, everything
has already been purchased. What can I do?*

A: First, your friends or relatives who've been getting married must know some very
generous people. In all my years in this business, I've yet to come across a gift wish list
on which everything is accounted for. What is more likely, for me and probably for lots
of other people, is that all the gifts in your *price range* have been spoken for, so you're
left with getting either the $12.99 corkscrew or the $500 bone china serving platter.
So, what do you do? Get creative.

Let's take that $12.99 corkscrew for openers. On its own, it seems awfully measly,
but if you add other wine-related gifts to it, it'll be awesome. If I were facing a registry
list with only the corkscrew left on it, I'd buy the corkscrew, but then I'd invest in a case
of good wine, four amazing wine glasses, and maybe a wine rack or wine cooler. Or
how about this? If the couple lives in a region known for its wine, buy the corkscrew,
but then put it in a box along with a reservation for a weekend in the nearby wine
country. Eastern Long Island in New York and California's Napa Valley are two areas
known for their wine making. Finally, certain wineries across the country will create
personalized labels on bottles of wine so that you can, in essence, create your own vintage. Along with the corkscrew, give them a case of wine in which every bottle has a
label that wishes them congratulations or bears their names and their wedding date.
(Three vineyards that do custom labeling—Chaddsford Winery, New Hope Winery,
and Windsor Vineyards—are described in Chapter 7.)

Another way to get creative is to use the already-filled registry list as a guide to
other gifts that will coordinate with the stuff on the registry. The fact that the items
have already been purchased doesn't mean you can't look at them. For example, go
see firsthand the kinds and colors of linens that the bride and groom registered for. If,
for example, the couple is going for a Western theme, with denim slipcovers and ban-

dana print pillows, buy them some Western-inspired housewares, such as coasters in the shape of a sheriff's star or hurricane lamps that look as if they'd be at home on the range. Or if the registry indicates a more retro look, log on to eBay or visit a local antiques fair for cool glasses, serving bowls, or vases that will go with those items.

Size Up Housewares

When you're not working from a registry list, you're still safe with a housewares gift: a cheery pottery serving bowl, a pair of candlesticks and a box of decorative candles—you get the picture. Everyone has a use for gifts such as these, regardless of how often the couple entertains. For example, in my home, we tend to keep the breakables on the top shelves of our entertainment center because of our two active children. But look there and you'll find all of the glassware, serving bowls, and candlesticks we've received over the years. They add a decorative flair to the furnishings, and when we entertain, we put them to good use.

There are plenty of these types of gifts in any one of the national housewares retailers—Bed, Bath & Beyond, Pier One, or Crate & Barrel, to name a few. I also like to shop in unique boutiques, like the one in my town that carries Fiestaware pieces and one-of-a-kind pottery. My favorite gift to buy there is supersize coffee mugs, like the ones used at Central Perk on "Friends." I drink these up because they're conducive for someone who drinks coffee as well as someone who doesn't—they can hold hot chocolate, tea, pencils, or can simply decorate a shelf.

TLC for the Bride-to-Be

When in doubt, gifts that pamper are always well received. If there's anything that's true about a busy bride-to-be, it's that she doesn't slow down often enough to give herself some tender loving care. Thus, when she receives a gift that's all about pampering, she will immediately think, "Hey, when can I use this?" Two of my favorite pampering gifts over the years have been bath salts, which reintroduced me to the glory of soaking in a tub, and gift certificates for spa treatments.

For a package of gifts in this realm, look into the clever pampering "kits" on the market these days. They might come packaged in something cute, like a paint can, and include everything needed to turn an ordinary bathroom into a luxurious at-home spa: bath salts, body scrub, yummy scented lotions, a CD of soothing music, and an aromatherapy candle.

If you'd like to shower the bride with pampering time away from home, find out where she goes to get her hair cut or her favorite nail salon, and buy her a gift certificate for a manicure, scalp massage, or similar service. Or buy her a certificate for use at a place that you like and trust—that is, if you live near one another, of course. If you don't live close by or know much about pampering services, you can call

---

❧ *The Best Gift I Ever Got* ❧

At my bridal shower, I received a pair of hand-knit Christmas stockings. On the front of one was my name, and on the front of the other was my husband's name. On the back of each was our wedding date. It was such a thoughtful gift, and we continue to use these stockings every year at Christmas.

Laura, New York

SpaFinders at (800) ALL-SPAS (255-7727). This clearinghouse will help you pinpoint a reputable spa in the bride's hometown and purchase a gift certificate for a specific service.

Wedding Gifts—and Customs to Consider

Having grown up on the East Coast—New York, to be precise—I was raised to believe that when you go to a wedding, you hand the bride and groom a check, and you call it a day. This is how I routinely congratulated friends and family when they tied the knot, and no one ever gave it a second thought. Then, shortly after Bill and I were married, we moved to Michigan so Bill could attend graduate school. While there, we made friends with many couples and were invited to several weddings. It was just before the first of those weddings that I happened to be discussing gifts with another woman and mentioned that I was planning on giving the happy couple a check. Her face froze, her jaw dropped, and she gasped, "You're going to do what?"

"Give them money," I repeated.

"Why don't you just slap them in the face instead?" she suggested.

∼❧ The Best Gift I Ever Got ❧∼

For our wedding, my husband's two sisters gave us an antique pine writing table, which I still have today. It's a unique piece, and I still look at it and remember sitting there and writing all of my thank-you notes.

Kathleen, Pennsylvania

> ⇜ *The Best Gift 1 Ever Gave* ⇝
>
> I like to give gifts with a theme for bridal showers, and my favorite of late
> is this one: a pizza stone, plus other pizza-making tools, topped off with
> a cookbook filled with unique ways to make a pizza pie.
>
> *Mandy, California*

After my own jaw dropped, I asked her to explain. I suddenly felt like a foreigner in a foreign land. After a quick lesson on local customs I learned that while money was an acceptable—if not the preferred—gift for brides and grooms in the Northeast, in the Midwest that was not so. When you arrive at a Midwest wedding, you bring a box, not an envelope. Giving a gift of money *is* seen as a slap in the face, and only the most insensitive guests just write a check. I also learned that according to local etiquette, your first course of action is to buy the bride and groom a gift off their registry. If the couple is not registered, then your second option is to buy something nice from the china or housewares section of the local department store. Your third option—well, there really isn't one, since money is out of the question, so you should make option one or two work.

At that time, I was just starting my career as a wedding writer and gift-giving adviser. The last thing I wanted to do was commit a social faux pas at my first Midwest wedding so I adjusted my gift giving accordingly.

For the first wedding, I headed to my local department store (at the time, Hudson's), found the couple's registry, and bought a handful of the silver flatware they'd requested. For the next wedding, I went back to Hudson's, got the registry, and secured six pieces of the crystal they'd designated. The wedding after that, for which the couple had also registered at Hudson's, I went for two place settings of their china. Each of those gifts were happily accepted by the newlyweds, and I came away with a better appreciation of the gift registry's role in facilitating the gift-giving process.

The most important lesson I learned from my Midwest experience was this: You must know the customs and etiquette that apply in the area where you'll be attending a wedding, and keep them in mind when selecting a gift. If you're a New Yorker flying to Texas for a wedding, do your homework prior to settling on a gift. Find out if money is OK to give at a Texas wedding before you hand over the check. If it's not, get yourself a copy of the couple's registry so you can make a socially correct choice. After attending weddings nationwide, I've concluded that a gift from the registry is more widely accepted than a gift of money. So, if there's a shadow of a doubt (even in the Northeast), you can give a gift with confidence if you stick with the couple's registry.

Finally, even if you don't attend a wedding to which you're invited, you should still send a gift. Etiquette rules state that you have up to a year after the wedding to do so, but I think it's best to do it right away—almost as soon as you receive the invitation and send back your regrets.

Bonus Gift-Giving Section

Giving a gift often involves just shopping at the mall. Maybe you'd like to do your shopping in cyberspace, or perhaps you're intent on gifts that benefit a good cause. Other times, you may want to send a gift that represents your hometown or your state mammal. And don't forget party favors for your guests. When it all comes together, they'll thank you for it.

This final chapter ties up these loose ends in five sections:

- Being a Smart Internet Shopper

- Gifts for Your Guests

- Gifts That Benefit a Good Cause

- Gifts of Place

- How to Write Thank-You Notes

Being a Smart Internet Shopper

I've been an avid on-line shopper since 1998. I've never had a problem with goods not being delivered or my credit card number being lifted. Then again, I tend to stick to the more mainstream sites at which I'm confident I'll be treated well. One electronic shopping venue I've yet to try is on-line auctions. If that's your preferred method of shopping on-line, you may want to hear about my friend Jamie who learned her lesson about how to shop (or bid) smartly on-line.

A Rude Introduction to On-Line Auctions

Jamie is a big fan of Eddie Izzard, the cross-dressing British comedian who has had several specials on HBO. Last fall, she was planning a dinner party and wanted to show a video of Izzard's antics as the evening's entertainment. The only problem: at that time, Izzard's performances weren't readily available in the United States. So, Jamie, who shops on-line at least once a month, visited Amazon.com's auctions in search of an Izzard tape. She found two, listed by a seller named "Mrs. Badcrumble." After bidding $71 and winning, Jamie eagerly sent a check to the seller, who cashed it in early November. By Christmas, Jamie still had no Eddie Izzard videos. (I think the seller's name should have been her first clue.)

Unfortunately, Jamie's tale of E-woe is common. You might think that the greatest potential for getting ripped off on-line comes from a hacker getting your credit card number from an E-tailer's website, but according to the National Consumers League, a nonprofit organization dedicated to consumer issues, on-line auctions have ranked number one for on-line fraud since 1997. The organization reports that of the six million shoppers on-line, only 7 percent experience fraud or misuse of credit card information. The real risk lies in paying with a check or money order, as Jamie can tell you.

Credit Cards Are a Must

As a matter of fact, the best way to ensure that you won't get fleeced on-line is to pay by credit card. If you have a problem with your transaction, the credit card company will go to bat for you to resolve it. If Jamie had paid with good old plastic, she might have been able to wield the muscle of MasterCard in getting Mrs. Badcrumble to cough up the goods. Moreover, while she was disputing the charge, she wouldn't have had to pay it. But once Mrs. Badcrumble cashed her check, her money was gone.

Nevertheless, on-line security is a difficult issue, and many shoppers are reluctant to use credit cards for electronic purchases. The best course is to err on the side of caution. Even though, statistically, most Web fraud does not involve credit cards, you can't be too careful when shopping on-line. Look for websites with the following must-have features:

A Secure Server

A secure server encrypts the data on the site to prevent inquiring minds and fraudulent fingertips from gaining access to your personal information, including your credit card number. How can you tell if an on-line merchant uses a secure server? First, read the site's security statement, which is usually located at the bottom of the home page. Second, look for two important pieces of information on the site itself: the plural URL and the lock.

The Plural URL. When you enter a site's secure server, look for a change in the URL (short for "uniform resource locator"—the website's address): the prefix of "http" will become "https."

Lock It Up. At the same time that the URL changes, you'll notice that the icon of a closed padlock or a key (depending on your browser) appears on the periphery of the page. This is another way for the site and your browser to let you know that you've entered a secure site.

If you don't see either of those "locked" icons or a change in the URL when you get to a page that asks you for private information, log out. You can't be sure the site has a secure server.

A Strict Privacy Policy

Keeping your credit card information secure shouldn't be your only concern when shopping on-line. Also make sure that any on-line retailer with which you want to do business has a privacy policy in place (look for the statement on the home page). The site should promise that it won't peddle your personal information, including E-mail address, to other on-line merchants. (This practice could lead to an E-mailbox filled with spam, or unwanted mail.)

A Good Track Record Is a Must

It's also wise to do some research and shop only on sites that have treated others well. For commentary on how various E-tailers have performed, go to BizRate.com, an independent rating company that surveys on-line buyers at the time they make a purchase—and again a week later when, ideally, the merchandise should have arrived. One site where I shop that uses BizRate.com is Staples.com (for office supplies). Whenever I complete an order, a BizRate window pops up and asks me to rate my shopping experience. This information is used to grade on-line merchants and award them anywhere from one to five gold stars. Currently, BizRate gives the lowdown on about three thousand sites.

A less technical way of sizing up an E-tailer is to ask people you know who shop on-line where they go to buy their stuff and how they've been treated there.

Place Your Trust in an Escrow Service

If shopping at regular E-tailers is too tame and you crave an on-line auction, be smart about how you pay. If plastic isn't an option, use an escrow service such as i-Escrow.com, which secures your money with a third party until you receive and review the goods. In addition, deal only with an auction site that will stand behind its services, as Amazon.com did with Jamie. She filed a complaint about "Mrs. Badcrumble," and shortly after Christmas, Amazon.com refunded her $71. While that made Jamie feel very good about Amazon.com—where she has continued to do her on-line shopping and bidding—it still left her wanting those Eddie Izzard videotapes.

Gifts for Your Guests

Along with the occasions when we thank our hosts with a gift, there are times when we, as the hosts, don't want to send our guests off empty-handed. People who attend your child's birthday party, your wedding, your baby shower, or a dinner party are all candidates for such recognition. When you want to make your guests feel special, use some of the ideas in this section for goodie bags, favors, and mementos.

Children's Birthday Parties

When my daughter Jane turned four, I created a party favor that held appeal for children and parents alike, because it was both practical and fun. I started with a stack of brightly colored twenty-eight-ounce plastic tumblers. Using sparkly paint pens, I wrote each child's name on one of the cups. Then, inside I put some candy, a bottle of bubbles, and either plastic jewelry and hair accessories for girls or drinking straws featuring *Star Wars* characters for boys. I wrapped the entire ensemble in clear cellophane and tied it with ribbon so that it looked a little like a festive pineapple. The end result? A professional-looking favor that cost just a few dollars each to make.

Other unusual ideas for birthday party favors include:

- Small tubs of Play-Doh and plastic cookie cutters

- Tie-dyed T-shirts that commemorate your child's birthday celebration

- Lunchbox-type containers packed with crayons and a coloring book, rubber stamps, stickers, or temporary tattoos

If the group is older, instead of toys, give each guest a gift bag with a store gift card inside. I usually recommend cards in a $10 denomination from the kinds of stores favored by preteens and teens—booksellers, video stores, electronics retailers, or mass merchants where there's some-

thing for everyone. Or give them a gift certificate to the local movie theater chain—basically, something they can enjoy using in their free time
and with their friends.

Wedding Receptions

Where I grew up, candy-covered almonds wrapped in tulle were the de
rigueur wedding favor. Sure, guests eat them up, but when you want to
buck tradition, consider the following suggestions:

- Freshly potted seasonal flowers or plants, such as a poinsettia for
  a December wedding or a pot of petunias for a spring wedding

- Votive candles

- A small box of chocolates or a cluster of Hershey's Kisses wrapped
  in pretty fabric or enclosed in foil gift bags

- Small picture frames, which can double as holders for seat assign-
  ment cards

- Personalized bottles of wine—buy by the case from a winery that
  will let you custom-design a label with your name and wedding
  date, and then offer these as a toast to your guests

- Souvenirs of the place where you were married—for example, if
  you hold a destination wedding in Hawaii, give each guest a fresh-
  flower lei. For a weekend wedding in Vermont, present them
  with fancy bottles of maple syrup in a brown bag decorated with
  pine-cone-shape stamps in silver and gold.

Baby Showers

It's always fun to throw an expectant mom a baby shower. You get to make a fuss over the roundness of her belly and laugh as everyone shares crazy cravings stories. Not only do you want to celebrate the upcoming arrival, you also want the women who attend to carry away a little treasure as well. Here are two suggestions for fun favors:

• *Notepaper.* You can buy off the rack in a card store, or opt for more distinguished stock—maybe pastel-colored cards that a local artist created. For a note of elegance, seek out cards that feature pressed flowers or prints from a local museum.

• *Anything pampering.* Give bath salts, hand creams, or sweet-smelling soaps, and attach a note that says you want your guests to "baby" themselves with this gift. Good sources of these kinds of pampering products are stores that sell Caswell-Massey and Lady Primrose brands, as well as spas and beauty salons.

Dinner Parties

I recently attended a dinner party given by a woman who is known around town for her out-of-this-world cookies. Whenever our children's school needs someone to bake cookies for class parties or fund-raisers, this woman steps up to the table—and leaves us hungry for more. She knows that everyone goes bonkers over her baked goods, and she likes to keep her fans salivating by not revealing the recipe. However, as dinner guests in her home, we were given a special treat to take home: a ball of refrigerated cookie dough, made from her coveted recipe, wrapped in red cellophane and tied with a white bow, from which a cookie cutter hung. While she didn't come clean on exactly how she makes her wonderful cookies, she did send us off with a sample of the batter so we could experience them fresh from the oven. I made that batch the next day with my daughters, and we were in heaven.

If you've earned a reputation for excelling at making something—cookies, a vegetable appetizer, fruit jam—send your dinner party guests home with individual samples of your culinary creation.

Or you can stick with more traditional favors, such as:

- Delicate candles, such as votives or ones that float

- Small, ornate picture frames

- Copies of that evening's menu printed on parchment, rolled into a scroll, and tied with a raffia ribbon; you can even personally inscribe each menu and convey your heartfelt thanks that the person joined you for dinner

- A wrapped package of chocolates or mints

For dinner parties where children are welcomed, have pint-size favors on hand as well, such as miniature race cars or colored pencils. For a New Year's Eve party we hosted, my daughters decorated brown paper lunch bags and filled them with candy, toys, and noisemakers. We gave them out to all the children who attended. When you remember your smallest guests with a little gift, you'll have happy children *and* parents.

Gifts That Benefit a Good Cause

Whenever possible, I like to send someone a gift that benefits a good cause. One avenue is buying items from local nonprofit or charitable organizations to help with their fund-raising. For example, this past year some of our family members received holiday decorations that students at my daughter's elementary school had made. The decorations looked professional, and the revenue helped support the school. On other occasions I might select an item that has been earmarked to support a specific cause, such as the pink candle that Avon was selling last year—part of the proceeds went to help fund breast cancer research.

There are hundreds, if not thousands, of other ways to buy gifts with redeeming value. Instead of listing them all here, I've highlighted a few stellar ones to consider the next time you want to buy a do-good gift. (If you want a thorough resource to gifts that benefit a good cause, I recommend two books by Ellen Berry: *Gifts That Make a Difference* and *Gifts That Save the Animals*, both from Foxglove Publishing.)

Berea College Crafts

You may remember this institution from Chapter 3. Berea College is a small, liberal-arts school in Berea, Kentucky, that has had a tuition-free policy since its founding in 1855. One of the ways the college supports itself and is able to offer free education to some 1,500 students is through its crafts program, in which students are asked to participate. This program offers apprenticeship opportunities for students to learn iron smithing and woodworking, among other skills. The decorative items they create—from blown glass to wind chimes—are unique, professionally constructed, gorgeous, and not terribly expensive. You can scroll through an extensive list of the items for sale on the college's website at bereacollegecrafts.com.

Museum Stores

I love visiting museums, but I'm even more of a connoisseur of their museum stores. I always find unique items, and I know my purchase helps support the facility and its collections. The two companies listed here have banded together with various museums to help them sell their wares worldwide.

Museum Tour

This Oregon company has a catalog and Web presence at museum-tour.com. Currently, it sells items from twenty-three museums or educational institutions across the country, from the Museum of Science in Boston to the Los Angeles County Museum of Art. Museum Tour's offerings lean toward educational toys for kids, but many items are meant for grown-ups, including Edgar Degas–inspired pins from the Art Institute of Chicago and silk scarves featuring Texas bluebonnet flowers from Fort Worth's Amon Carter Museum.

MuseumShop.com

This Web-based business, also cited in Chapter 2, offers a worldwide collection of museum-inspired wares from sixty institutions, including the Vatican Library, the Louvre, and the Israel Museum. Closer to home, you can find items from museums in the lower forty-eight, such as the Brooklyn Museum of Art, Mystic Seaport in Connecticut, and the Minneapolis Institute of Arts.

Heifer Project International

The mission of this charitable organization harks back to the saying "Give a man a fish, and he eats for a day; teach a man to fish, and he eats for a lifetime." A donation to Heifer Project International (HPI), made in the gift recipient's name, ensures the delivery of livestock of various species to a poor family in a poverty-stricken area of the world. You can buy a gift of bees for a family in Ghana for $30, or give a South American family a llama for $150. Since 1944, HPI has helped more than four million families in 118 countries become self-reliant by providing them with farm animals—and training about how to use them to support a family. For a catalog call (800) 422-0474 or go to heifer.org on the Web.

World Vision International

Like HPI, this humanitarian organization lets you buy livestock for poor families, but it also offers opportunities to support those who are less fortunate in ways that go beyond commerce. For example, for $24 you can buy a year's worth of supplies for schoolchildren in Africa; $40 will cover toys to be used on a Romanian orphanage's playground; or $20 will immunize a child in India against six childhood diseases. Stateside, you can give $35 toward the purchase of new winter coats for some of America's poorest children. Not all of the gift opportunities are child-centered: you can also purchase a plow and two oxen for a Malawian farmer in Africa for $450. Like HPI, you can give a gift in someone's name. To order a gift catalog, call (888) 511-6511, or visit the World Vision International website at worldvisiongifts.org.

Gifts of Place

Sometimes the best gift to give someone, regardless of the occasion, is what I call a "gift of place"—an item for which a city or state is best known. These gifts let you memorialize the place where you live, a place where the gift recipient once lived, or a place to which you've traveled.

When we lived in Michigan, our gift of choice on most holidays was anything that featured the maize and blue of the University of Michigan, where my husband was attending graduate school. Whenever we traveled to northern Michigan, famed locally for its annual cherry festival, we'd return home with cherry-related products to give as gifts. Other times, we might give a gift representative of the automobile industry, a cornerstone of Michigan's economy.

If your gift giving is all over the map, consult the following state-by-state guide for items that best embody the places you—or the gift recipient—hold dear.

Alabama

A lot of foods originate in Alabama, including pecans (the state's official nut), Gulf Coast seafood, and muscadine grapes, an especially hearty grape variety that thrives in the southeastern United States. Look for jellies, juices, and wine made from these grapes for a luscious Alabama gift.

Alaska

Since Alaska is well known for its native people, a gift of indigenous arts and crafts is a top choice. Additional items to look for include decorative items made from scrimshaw or anything representing Eskimo culture, such as an ulu knife (pronounced "oo-loo"), which has a hatchetlike blade with a handle attached to the top. This knife dates back more than five thousand years and is still considered one of the best cutting tools in native Alaskan households.

Arizona

Arizona is graced with one of the world's natural wonders—the Grand Canyon—and a gift that shows its majestic beauty, such as a photograph or painting, would be an excellent choice. The fabled Route 66 also runs through the Grand Canyon State, so keep your eyes peeled for items representing road travel. Also be on the lookout for anything with the saguaro cactus on it, which happens to be the namesake of one of Arizona's national parks.

Arkansas

The mascot of the University of Arkansas is the Razorback, so a gift emblazoned with this wild pig should make an Arkansas fan go hog wild. With the Ozark National Forest near the northwest corner of the state, you'd also want to give an Ozark-crafted item. Whatever you do, pass up the temptation to give any Bill Clinton gag gifts.

California

Several major icons beckon in the Golden State—the Golden Gate Bridge, Yosemite National Park, Hollywood, and the mighty redwood trees—gifts featuring them should be readily available. In addition, California's renowned wine country, encompassing the Napa and Sonoma Valleys, naturally suggests the gift of spirits. Souvenirs from the state's popular sports attractions are also good picks; these range from Rose

Bowl paraphernalia to gear from the California Angels, Oakland A's, or Los Angeles Dodgers.

Colorado

Colorado has more mountains of high elevation than any other state in the country. No wonder there's a profile of a mountain range on the Rocky Mountain State's license plate. That should put gifts related to the mountains or the skiing areas of Aspen, Breckenridge, or Boulder high on your list. On a more individual level, even though Colorado is land-locked, Denver was the home of the Unsinkable Molly Brown, a much-storied *Titanic* survivor. There's a museum in Denver where you're sure to find nifty Molly Brown memorabilia. Also look for jewelry made with aquamarine, the state's gemstone.

Connecticut

Connecticut's Mystic Seaport and its magnificent ships are sure to inspire a nautical gift that's right on course. You may be surprised to learn that "Yankee Doodle" is Connecticut's state song; so a musical gift might be a music box or a novelty item playing this ditty. Finally, the robin, sperm whale, and praying mantis are all official "wildlife" of the Constitution State, giving you an eclectic family of gift possibilities.

Delaware

As with many other East Coast states, Delaware's beaches draw thousands of tourists every year, so gifts of hand-painted buoys, lighthouse replicas, or anything with a nautical theme get a wave of approval. Barring those, the ladybug is the state insect, so anything incorporating this cute little bug would make a whimsical remembrance. If you want something historical and related to business, buy something made from nylon, since this fabric was first made in Delaware by DuPont.

District of Columbia

Anywhere you turn in our nation's capital, you're a stone's throw from landmarks and museums, all of which are excellent sources for gifts, souvenirs, and memorabilia—such as models of the White House or the Washington Monument.

Florida

One of the most wholesome gifts from the Sunshine State is one of its principal crops: oranges. There's Disney World, Universal Studios, and Sea World for kitschy or kid-related gifts. Something with an alligator theme, or, for the sports buff, Gatorade, which was developed at the University of Florida, are fun Florida gifts as well. Local artists in the Florida Keys or Miami can be a source of seascape-inspired art, or you can acquire compositions of a different kind—Tom Petty music or Dave Barry books. Both masters of their crafts are from Florida.

Georgia

They don't call Georgia the Peach State because of its shape: peaches are one of its top crops, along with peanuts, and both are popular food gifts. Want something with a longer shelf life? With the duo of Coca-Cola and CNN based here, you've also got your pick of products featuring the logos of these two business behemoths. *Gone with the Wind* was set in Atlanta, and fanciers of Southern culture go crazy for anything having to do with this timeless classic. Finally, if you move fast enough, you can find some leftover Olympic memorabilia for those who collect that kind of stuff.

Hawaii

Gifts from Hawaii to keep an eye out for include: anything with a picture of a pineapple on it or food with a pineapple flavor; macadamia nuts; locally grown Kona coffee; a hand-crafted ukulele; a grass skirt; an authentic flower lei; or one of those fabulously gaudy Hawaiian shirts.

Idaho

There are three things for which Idaho is known—and they are ideal resources for gifts from this state: potatoes (Idaho supplies nearly two-thirds of all potatoes in the United States); pine trees (the state has more white pines than any other state); and silver.

Illinois

As the Land of Lincoln, Illinois boasts two Lincoln landmarks: his home in Springfield, which is now a National Historic Site, and his burial place, also in Springfield. Not surprisingly, Springfield, the most visited place in the state, is the spot to find Lincoln memorabilia. Of course, Illinois is also home to the Windy City, Chicago, where options range from gifts from myriad shops along the Magnificent Mile to items depicting Chicago landmarks to souvenirs embellished with the various sports teams' logos. In addition, there's local music (Chicago blues) and, of course, Wrigley's gum (the company is headquartered in Chicago).

Indiana

Talk about your culture clashes. You can give gifts from Indiana that run the gamut from Mennonite crafts or furniture to mementos from the Indianapolis Motor Speedway. Residents of the Hoosier State are rabid sports fans (think of the movie *Hoosiers*), so anything done up in the red and white of Indiana University scores big. Finally, if you're can't resist a gag gift, remember that David Letterman is a native son—take his off-beat humor as your inspiration.

Iowa

Corn is big business here in the Hawkeye State, and gift buyers have plenty of related merchandise to capture the Iowa experience. For snack lovers, you have giant vats of popcorn. For nap lovers, there are even shops that sell corn pillows! Each year, the Iowa State Fair is a big deal and is wide open for buying presents as well.

Kansas

The official symbols of Kansas include sunflowers, bison, and wheat, and the state song is "Home on the Range." Movie buffs will always think of this territory as the setting for *The Wizard of Oz*. "I've a feeling we're not in Kansas anymore," Dorothy mused to Toto in the film; so memorabilia of both the book and the film should blow them away.

Kentucky

One of the best-known, locally made products from Kentucky is the Louisville Slugger, and the factory is open for tours and abuts an excellent museum on baseball history. Both are home-run sources for gifts. In addition, all horse-racing eyes turn to the Bluegrass State each year for the Kentucky Derby, a source of gift inspiration for horse lovers everywhere.

Louisiana

A gift of beads or anything else representing Mardi Gras in New Orleans will make someone's day. For something a bit spicier, take advantage of the state's rich Cajun heritage: give 'em a gumbo-making kit (a big pot, spices, and a Louisiana-inspired cookbook) or a bottle of Tabasco (residents' favorite condiment). Also among the possibilities are CDs of Dixieland jazz or the Neville Brothers, and coffee or beignet mix from Café du Monde in New Orleans.

Maine

If you want to make someone who lives (or used to live) in Maine happy, send them lobsters. If you were hoping for something more subtle than a red-shelled crustacean, sail over — anytime — to the venerable retail institution L.L.Bean in Freeport, which is known worldwide for staying open twenty-four hours a day. Give the Maine lover on your list anything featuring a moose, chickadee, or Maine coon cat—all official state animals—and you'll make these Yankees proud. Author Stephen King is a prominent resident and is also an avid supporter of reading and the arts in the Pine Tree State. Choose from among his many titles for a gift that will send chills down the reader's spine.

Maryland

Crabs or anything else in a seafood vein—Chesapeake clam sauce, for example—are good gifts. Or, cast your net over the art inspired by the seascapes on Maryland's eastern shore. Big-city Baltimore has an outstanding aquarium, and don't forget Camden Yards, home of baseball's Baltimore Orioles. You'll find sporting gifts for kids and kids at heart at both places.

Massachusetts

For a small New England state, Massachusetts gives you plenty of gift options—from artist colonies in the western part of the state (the Norman Rockwell museum is here) to fishing communities along the Bay State's two capes, Cape Cod and Cape Ann. There's also the Boston area, which is rich in Colonial memorabilia for the history buffs on your list as well as home to the perennial underdogs, the Boston Red Sox. With its concentration of colleges, Massachusetts is a mecca for getting collegiate memorabilia and attire: there's Harvard, MIT, Boston University, Wellesley, Smith, Williams, and Boston College, just to name a few. Walden Pond can inspire a thoughtful gift for literary souls, and for mouth-watering choices there are Boston baked beans and anything with cranberries in it.

Michigan

You can't go wrong if you send something featuring the green and white of Michigan State's Spartans or the maize and blue of the University of Michigan's Wolverines. Just make sure to check where your gift recipients' allegiances lie. Sending something green to a Wolverines fan or something blue and gold to a Spartans fan may be grounds for dissolving a friendship. If you want to play it safe, Michigan has the most coastline of any state except for Alaska, so you can comb the shores for items related to water sports or fishing. For music buffs and automobile enthusiasts, there are always goods about Motown or the car industry.

Minnesota

Here in the home of the Mall of America, the country's largest shopping mall, you shouldn't have a problem buying a gift. Garrison Keillor of "Prairie Home Companion" is based here, and you can please radio and music devotees with his works. Gastronomically speaking, Minnesota has two official foods: the blueberry muffin and the morel mushroom. Other marketable products of the state include Minnetonka moccasins and former wrestler, now governor, Jesse Ventura.

Mississippi

The magnolia is the state's official flower and tree, and it's a beloved symbol here as is anything with an antebellum theme. In the edibles category, a box of pecan turtles will win the day. (Don't worry: they're chocolates shaped like turtles.) Or choose a work by or about one of the state's native sons: Elvis Presley (Tupelo), William Faulkner (New Albany), or Tennessee Williams (Columbus). For those who like cutting-edge music, you've got the up-and-coming band North Mississippi All-Stars.

Missouri

The Show-Me State is the place that inspired Samuel Clemens, a.k.a. Mark Twain, what with the Mississippi River and all. Today, besides the landmark St. Louis Arch, many people identify Missouri with Branson, arguably the state's entertainment capital—and a close second to Nashville, Tennessee, as a lightning rod for country music–inspired performers. Missouri is also home to Anheuser-Busch and the St. Louis Cardinals.

Montana

Thanks to the film *A River Runs Through It*, Montana evokes images of fly-fishing for many folks. And anglers will thank you for your gift of fly-fishing gear or other items related to the sport. Another hook is anything having to do with the vast openness of the state, which is why it's called Big Sky Country. While Helena is the state's official capital, Missoula is probably Montana's cultural and shopping capital and is home to the state's arboretum—a great source of botanical bounty.

Nebraska

Nebraska is where much of Old West history was made—from Lewis and Clark to the Pony Express. As in Iowa, there's nothing like corn for a locally grown or made gift, such as popcorn on the cob. Omaha Steaks is also based in the Cornhusker State. Here's one for the trivia books and inspiration for a cool kitschy gift: Kool-Aid was created in Hastings, Nebraska, in the 1920s and is the state's official soft drink. You can serve up some of this refreshment for a sweet treat.

Nevada

Take a gamble on Las Vegas–themed gifts (think lounge acts like Wayne Newton and Liberace) or items made of locally mined gemstones or metals, including opal, turquoise, and silver. Nevada residents are sweet on Ethel M chocolate, whose factory you can tour in nearby Henderson and pick up sweets for all. (By the way, the M stands for the Mars company, maker of M&Ms candy.) Speaking of Mars, Nevada is also home to the infamous Area 51, a hotbed for alleged alien activities and UFO sightings. Pick up a souvenir featuring little green men for anyone you know who is an *X-Files* fan and believes "the truth is out there."

New Hampshire

New Hampshire is best known for its White Mountains, part of the Appalachian Trail and crowned by Mount Washington. Many cars in the Northeast display bumper stickers bragging that the vehicle climbed Mount Washington, and these insignia make great kitschy gifts. You can't go wrong with a sample of the locally produced maple syrup or maple candies; for waistline watchers, beeswax candles are another New Hampshire hallmark. And you'll find fantastic outlet shopping in North Conway, where you can pick up great gifts for the home at furniture maker Yield House.

New Jersey

Most Jersey-ites love the Garden State's native musical son, Bruce Springsteen, so anything by him will be a hit. For collectors, steer toward memorabilia of Atlantic City—the heyday of casinos, or the Miss America pageant—or anything having to do with Thomas Edison, who did his inventing in New Jersey. A sweet gift is some saltwater taffy, which was first made in New Jersey years ago. If you're going for a gag, get anything that represents the state's two major (and much maligned) highways: the Garden State Parkway and the New Jersey Turnpike.

New Mexico

Like its neighbor Arizona, New Mexico is one of the states that Route 66 crosses, which is your guide for a number of possible gifts. Old gas station signs? T-shirts or pins with a Route 66 image? Models of classic cars—the kind that people drove before the Interstate Highway system made Route 66 itself a relic? Other landmarks in New Mexico include Carlsbad Caverns and the Roswell area. Capital Santa Fe is synonymous with Native American arts and crafts and is also home to the Georgia O'Keeffe Museum. For those whose taste goes more to food, New Mexican traditionally means hot and spicy, as in red and green chiles.

New York

Much of what people think of as being in a New York state of mind comes from the downstate part of the Empire State: fresh bagels and bialys, New York cheesecake, Times Square, Broadway, subway cars, yellow cabs, the Statue of Liberty, and the Brooklyn Bridge. But beyond New York City, the state is also home to Niagara Falls (and all of its touristy trinkets) and many notable colleges and universities: Cornell, Columbia, Culinary Institute of America, Vassar, NYU, and more. The vegetarian in your life will drool over a Moosewood cookbook, based on a popular vegetarian restaurant in Ithaca. New York also makes headlines for its Rome apples and Long Island wine.

North Carolina

What put North Carolina on the map in the minds of many folks was the Wright Brothers' flying machine, which first left the ground at Kitty Hawk—and earned the state the right to put "First in Flight" on the license plate. Turning from the wild blue yonder back to the turf, gift options include merchandise related to the Tar Heels of the University of North Carolina and the other big basketball school down the road from Raleigh—Duke University. Residents and visitors to the state also bask in many natural beauties, the big three being the Outer Banks, the Great Smoky Mountains, and the Blue Ridge Parkway.

North Dakota

Good gifts to choose include items that capture the early history of the Dakotas and any of the wholesome foods made from locally grown ingredients, such as chokecherries, durum wheat, barley, corn, soybeans, and sunflower seeds. Residents of the Sioux State are proud of their Native American heritage, as they are of the North Dakota Museum of Art in Grand Forks.

Ohio

Two architectural landmarks in the Buckeye State inspire Ohio-related gifts: the Rock and Roll Hall of Fame and Museum (Cleveland) and the Longaberger Basket Company (Newark). With its I. M. Pei–designed glass triangular structure jutting from the edge of Lake Erie, the Hall of Fame is an imposing sight. Inside, you'll find chart-topping souvenirs to make a music lover happy. Due east of the capital city of Columbus, you can't miss the corporate headquarters of Longaberger: the building is shaped like one of the picnic baskets the company sells. These sturdy beauties are made of high-quality hardwood maples, and each is signed and dated on the bottom by the artisan. Naturally enough, they're a classic collector's item.

Oklahoma

Oklahoma has the largest concentration of Native Americans—about sixty different tribes—of any state, making Native American crafts an outstanding gift to give. Another is material related to native son Will

Rogers. Oklahoma is also known for some of its baked goods, including products of the Shawnee Milling Company; visit the corporate headquarters in Shawnee for cooking- and baking-related gifts. Another food-related landmark is in Oklahoma City: Famous Mel's Sandwich & Bake Shop; go there to buy mouth-watering cinnamon rolls.

Oregon

The beauty of nature gives Oregon its grandeur—and its residents pride. There's the country's deepest lake, Crater Lake, surrounded by dense forests. There's also the rugged Pacific coastline and its awe-inspiring cliffs. Like many other western states, Oregon is a place to be active, whether it be kayaking down the Columbia River or climbing Mount Hood. Put it all together with a gift that embraces the outdoors. Another memorial of the Beaver State would be anything featuring this official animal. Oregon also produces some diverse foods, including Tillamook cheeses, marionberry jams and jellies, and hazelnuts.

Pennsylvania

The Keystone State is steeped in Colonial and Revolutionary history—from Washington's Crossing of the Delaware to the Liberty Bell—which constitutes a broad category of memorable gifts. Another way to go back in time is via Lancaster County, which is Amish country and thus a repository of Amish-made furniture and crafts. Pennsylvanians are also praised for their food, and the smorgasbord of packaged treats from companies headquartered here includes Hershey candies, Herr's potato chips, and Tastycake snack cakes. You can also walk away with an original Philly cheese steak or Pennsylvania Dutch pretzel. Finally, a souvenir of any of the three P's—Pittsburgh, Philadelphia, and the Poconos—would be a good choice.

Rhode Island

Rhode Island is a tiny state, but there's a lot going on here. To whet your whistle, the Ocean State has two official drinks—lemonade and coffee milk—both of which make refreshing gifts. Rhode Island is also where you'll find the stately mansions of Newport and the origins of the game of lawn tennis. Each year, great tunes flood the Newport Jazz Festival. For food gifts that hit the spot, there's johnnycake meal and Rhode Island quahogs (a shellfish). And toy classic Mr. Potato Head recently became Rhode Island's unofficial mascot, mostly because the toy's creator, Hasbro, Inc., is headquartered in Providence.

South Carolina

A unique treat from South Carolina is ChocRoaches—semisweet chocolate replicas of the palmetto bug, the "Unofficial State Bird of South Carolina." For a more historical angle on food, pick up books on Low Country cooking from Hoppin' John's, a culinary bookstore in Charleston. Also in Charleston is the annual Spoleto Festival, which brings more dance, music, and culture to the state than residents can handle. Sweetgrass baskets are a pretty local craft to buy. And of course, here in the South, you're surrounded by items on the Civil War.

South Dakota

As corny as it may sound, one of the biggest doings in South Dakota is the Corn Palace, a convention center of sorts where locals go for concerts and sporting events. What makes the Corn Palace a novelty is its exterior mural, a tribute to South Dakota agriculture that is constructed of the products it heralds: corn, wheat, wild oats, rye, and more. Other good gift ideas include books and photos documenting the area's natural and manmade sites, such as the Black Hills, the Badlands, and Mount Rushmore. Since South Dakota is steeped in Native American traditions, items from the Sioux Nation, such as dream catchers and medicine bags, are also laudable.

Tennessee

There is a wide range of music in Tennessee, and anything connected with tune towns such as Memphis (birthplace of the blues) or Nashville (more than one hundred record labels are here) will make a fun gift. You could also focus your gift giving on local attractions such as Dollywood, the Grand Ole Opry, or Graceland, the king of the state's draws. Or look to the Women's Basketball Hall of Fame in Knoxville or the Jack Daniel Distillery in Lynchburg.

Texas

In the Lone Star State, you'll have a gift recipient dancing the two-step with anything that is Texas-shape, features a cowboy boot, or shows the armadillo (the official small mammal), Texas longhorn (official large mammal), or bluebonnet (official flower). Did you know that the official state dish of Texas is chili? Women called chili queens whipped up the first batches of the mouth-burning stuff in San Antonio some 150 years ago, and it's still beloved by residents and visitors today. Texans are also proud of the part they played in the space missions of yesteryear, so the Houston Space Center and its logo items are a continual draw here. If you want to give something big and bright from Texas, go for a Lone Star cut of blue topaz, the state's gem, which creates a single star in the middle of the stone. And of course, there's the omnipresent cowboy hat.

Utah

Two recent happenings that have put Utah on the map (beyond the Osmonds, Brigham Young University, and the Great Salt Lake) are Robert Redford's Sundance Film Festival and the announcement of the 2002 winter Olympics. Both provide great gift ideas. Skiing is world-class here, so perhaps the ski bum in your life would like something from Park City. Utah is the Beehive State, named more for the industriousness of its settlers than a proliferation of honey making. Still, you can run with the idea by choosing an authentic bee skep or, in a tamer nature, something made from honey.

Vermont

While Vermont is a state of independent thinkers, where preserving individuals' rights to live as they like is paramount, it is also a place where you can get some really good stuff to eat. Here among the prolific Vermont dairy farms, Ben & Jerry struck ice-cream gold. You can tour the company's factory near Burlington and lick some souvenirs of your own. Likewise, Green Mountain Coffee, which took its name from the state's national forest, delivers an excellent brew. You can also get awesome maple syrup and maple rock candy, and don't forget to pick up a box or two of Lake Champlain chocolates.

Virginia

Dating back as far as Jamestown, Virginia is one of the places that helped get America on its feet, and the state is imbued with history—from the American Revolution to the Civil War. Circle Williamsburg for period costumes and crafts, Charlottesville for relics of Thomas Jefferson, and the cities outside of Washington, D.C. for a more modern slice of history. On the natural order, there are the shores of Virginia Beach and the peaks of the Blue Ridge and Shenandoah Mountains.

Washington

For those with an affinity for the Seattle area, products that revolve around the city's Pike Street Market or the Space Needle are crowd pleasers. A fit for outdoorsy types is something from Mount Rainier National Park. Walla Walla onions hail from Washington, as do Washington State apples, and both go down nicely as food gifts. Or salute local talent past and present with media by or about Jimi Hendrix, Kurt Cobain, or Dale Chihuly, a contemporary artist who works in glass and hails from Tacoma. Flag anything with the logo of Redmond-based Microsoft as gifts for techies.

West Virginia

West Virginia is a haven for white-water rafting—especially on the New River in the southern part of the state. The state's ultra-luxurious Greenbrier Hotel is a chic place to purchase pampering gifts. West Virginia is considered the Mountain State: two mountain ranges grace its borders— the Appalachians and the Alleghenys—and its motto is "Mountaineers Always Free." This state was forever memorialized in John Denver's song "Take Me Home, Country Roads."

Wisconsin

If you want to make a Wisconsin resident smile, say "cheese." This is America's Dairyland, where the populace proudly refer to themselves as "cheese heads." Give a Green Bay Packers fan a hat shaped like a wedge of cheese, or a University of Wisconsin Badgers follower anything decked with this official state animal. Oshkosh B'Gosh and Lands' End, both of which are headquartered here, are great sources for fashion conscious givers and receivers. For crafts think of Door County, which sticks out into the western shores of Lake Michigan and sometimes is referred to as the Cape Cod of the Midwest.

Wyoming

When you see that bison waving on the Wyoming state flag, you know you've found the perfect icon for a gift. Wyoming is very much a western state, where cowboy gear rules, wagon trains once rolled, and legends such as Buffalo Bill Cody and Calamity Jane once lived. It is also home to Jackson Hole, a popular ski town, and Yellowstone National Park, with its famous geyser Old Faithful. For an authentic food gift, try smoked meats or "Cowboy Coffee," a Jackson Hole java maker.

How to Write Thank-You Notes

A recurring complaint I get about giving and receiving is: Why don't people write thank-you notes anymore? I've heard from wedding guests who marveled that the bride and groom never acknowledged their gifts, and business executives who were dismayed that associates didn't take the time to send a handwritten thank-you note. Sure, E-mail is speedier and easier, but I'm a stickler for certain social rules, and writing a brief but heartfelt note to acknowledge a gift is fundamental.

While my mother drilled me early on about the whys and hows of the thank-you note—and I'm passing that instruction along to my daughters—I've come to realize that one reason so many people don't send thank-you notes has nothing to do with being rude, ungrateful, or lazy. Rather, it's because they were never taught *how* to do it, so they're intimidated by the prospect—and they let that fear paralyze them into doing nothing.

If you happen to be among those citizens for whom composing a thank-you note doesn't come naturally, these concluding pointers will have you writing in no time.

Invest in Nice Stationery or Notepaper

First and foremost, you can't prepare to write a notable note without nice stationery or notepaper on which to write. Just as I stock up on all-occasion gifts for my gift closet, I keep a supply of notepaper on hand that I can use for personal correspondence. I sometimes buy cards on sale that actually say "Thank you" on the front, but just as often, I buy generic cards that I like and that would be suitable for the purpose. When I get a gift unexpectedly, I don't have to make a special trip to the store or make do with a sheet from a legal pad. While I do it the old-fashioned way, if you're technically inclined, you can create personalized notepaper on your computer and then print it out on a specialty stock from a stationery or office supplies store.

Get Organized

If you're the guest of honor at an event, or anytime you'll be receiving a large number of gifts in a short period of time—such as at a bridal shower, a birthday party, or even Christmas—it's critical to keep a running list of who gave you what. Jot down the name of the giver, the specific gift, and any brief positive thoughts or feelings that jump into your head as you open it. This list will help you in two ways: it will prevent you from forgetting anyone when you write out your thank-yous (crossing off the names as I go gives me an added sense of accomplishment), and incorporating the thoughts you recorded earlier lets you personalize each message.

Log Off: It Must Be Handwritten

I know how easy it would be to cut-and-paste some quickie thank-you notes in a word processing program or E-mail message, but a computer-generated note just doesn't have the same effect as a handwritten one. So, always take the time to write it longhand.

If you're helping a young child send a thank-you note, write the body yourself as you recite it aloud together, and then have the child "sign" his or her name. Don't worry if the letters in the signature are backwards or out of order. The fact that she personally signed it will mean more than you know to the gift giver who receives this missive in the mail.

Don't Overdo It

Here's a simple formula for writing a thank-you note that is personal, filled with emotion, and yet succinct:

1. Start by thanking the person for the specific gift. Begin by saying, "Dear Ginger: Thank you so much for the matched set of hats, gloves, and scarf" or "Dear Fred: Thank you for your generous check." When you identify the gift right up front, you're telling the giver that conveying personal thanks is important to you and that you're not just sending out generic thank-yous as a timesaver. Remember: the giver devoted time, thought, and money to you and your gift; you owe it to that person to at least write out a few phrases of gratitude.

2. Mention how you'll use the gift. In your next sentence, write something like "This set of winter accessories will keep me snug when I go outside to play with my kids." You want to communicate exactly how you'll be able to put the gift to use and why it's so perfect for your lifestyle. If you've received a gift of cash, explain what you hope to do with the money—even if it's just depositing it in a savings account for college. Say something like "I plan to use your check to help buy books at college" or "I'm going to use it to treat myself to a manicure."

3. Thank the giver again and finish the note. All you need to do is write one more line to say something like "Thanks again for the great gift and for remembering my birthday" and you're home free. Sign your name, and congratulate yourself for having just written a thank-you note with impressive style. Of course, if you want to add a few more lines before you sign, seal, and deliver it, that's OK, too.

4. Proofread your note before sending it. I can't tell you how many times I've written a thank-you note and put *your* for *you're* or made a similar mistake. Thank goodness I proof everything before I mail it. If you spot a mistake in your handiwork, fix it. You can write the correction right on

the note or, if you're feeling so inclined and you have enough stationery on hand, write the note over again. Tip: Be extra careful *not* to make the same error again. If you do rewrite, proofread the second version too, just to be sure.

What to Do About Gifts You Don't Like

You may wonder what you're supposed to do when you don't really like a gift you've received. I don't care if you return it to the store, give it to charity, or toss it in the trash—you still need to thank the gift giver. In this case, your second line of the thank-you note should focus on some redeeming quality of the gift, however small. For example, if someone gave you an ugly crystal duck, you could say something like "I love how sparkly the crystal gets when the sun hits it." Or, if someone gave you clothing that doesn't fit, isn't your color, or you would just never wear, say something like "I love the clothes from store X," which lets you get away with expressing your enthusiasm for the effort while making no mention per se of the article in question. If you can't find anything positive to say, at least attempt to offer a compliment: "It was one of the most creative gifts we received." The ideal here is to accomplish the task of thanking the giver without having to choke down any lies. (Be careful how you say "You shouldn't have!")

Time Is of the Essence

Now for the most important guideline: Regardless of what stationery you use or which adjective you choose to describe your gratitude, make sure you send your thank-you note within two weeks of receiving a gift. You'll be long remembered for your thoughtfulness.